Reach
for the Stars

Reach
for the Stars

Pursuing success through excellence

By Charles S. Lauer
Publisher, *Modern Healthcare*

CCI BOOKS
A division of Coffey Communications, Inc.
Walla Walla, Washington

Cover and book design by Steve Henderson

Library of Congress Catalog Card No. 96-085313

ISBN 1-881802-33-7

Dedication

To Cecil Coffey,

my mentor, who through his example
inspired me to reach for the stars.

You will always, sir, be in my heart.

Table of contents

SECTION I. Qualities for personal success

CHAPTER A. Inner qualities

CHAPTER B. Coping with stress and disappointment in the business world

SECTION II. Principles of success in action

PART 1. MAKING YOUR ORGANIZATION SHINE: SUCCESS IN
MANAGEMENT AND LEADERSHIP

CHAPTER A. Qualities of stellar managers and leaders

CHAPTER B. Avoiding black holes

CHAPTER C. Profiles in management and leadership excellence

. . . .

PART 2. REACHING THE CUSTOMER: SUCCESS IN SALES AND MARKETING

CHAPTER A. Qualities for success in sales

CHAPTER B. Getting the customer's attention—and what to do once you have it

 CHAPTER C. Profiles in sales and marketing excellence

PART 3. KEEPING THE CUSTOMER: SUCCESS IN CUSTOMER SERVICE

CHAPTER A. The essence of stellar customer service

CHAPTER B. Avoiding black holes

CHAPTER C. Profiles in customer service excellence

SECTION III. And then some . . .

Preface

YOU'RE DRIVING AT NIGHT on one of those desert highways without a curve for a hundred miles or more. To fend off fatigue, you pull over, get out, and stretch. Then you look up—and what you see is startling.

On this moonless and eerily silent night, far from the emissions-polluted atmosphere and lights of any city or town, the inky canopy above you is awash with billions of stars, stark in their brilliant clarity.

You're aware of a fleeting urge to reach out and touch them. Of course, everyone knows that reaching for the stars is a doomed and pointless effort.

Or is it?

The naysayers promised that man would never fly. They promised he would never orbit the earth. They promised he would never walk on the moon.

Now they vow he can never reach the stars. Even the nearest is too distant, they insist, given our most efficient means of propulsion.

But who's to say some future discovery might not solve that problem? One thing is certain: Man will never reach the stars if he doesn't first reach *for* them.

What's true in terms of space exploration is even truer in this shared adventure we call life. We never reach goals we don't first set. We never arrive if we don't set out for the destination. We never succeed if we don't aim for the star of success.

I've been a lifelong student of success—both personal and professional. I've studied those who have attained success in their relationships, in work, finances, personal habits, and character.

And I've discovered that certain predictable traits spell the difference between the ordinary and the extraordinary, between mediocrity and excellence, between the average and the superior, between existing and living, between drifting and achieving, between failure and success.

In this companion to my earlier book, *Soar With the Eagles* (CCI Books, 1991), it is again my privilege to share with you more secrets to success in life, in love, in work.

I'm convinced that anyone can be a success—and, of course, that includes you. You can achieve your dreams. To truly succeed, you'll undoubtedly need an attitude check. You'll consistently need to give more and do more than expected. You'll need to hone your skills in treating people with respect and in making them feel good about themselves.

Above all, you'll need to take action—to reach for the stars—and not merely to wish upon them.

Then, in the stillness of a desert night, you may finally yield to that compelling urge to reach toward the spangled sky, and lower your hand to find it filled with stardust.

Acknowledgments

THERE ARE SO MANY PEOPLE I would like to thank: Barbra Coffey, Alan Coffey, Jane Coffey, Richard and Barbara Kaplan, Kathryn Zahl, John Appleyard, Joyce Flory, George Conomikes, George Sheehan, M.D., Leonidas Nelson, David May, Cathy Fosco—and all my friends and colleagues.

Caring people inspire me. Life is so precious, and I have been fortunate enough to share many wonderful things with many wonderful friends.

I've been very lucky.

Introduction

REACH FOR THE STARS features a unique blend of practical sense and penetrating insight into how to achieve excellence and success in the business world.

In exploring the qualities necessary for success and presenting models of business excellence, *Reach for the Stars* encompasses a wide landscape. And it's that breadth which makes this book essential reading for anyone in—or thinking of entering—the demanding world of business. Whether you're a top-flight executive, head of a small customer service department, an aspiring salesperson, or an experienced manager currently between jobs, this book is for you.

If you're a business novice, standing on the shore with your toes dipping into the water, ready to plunge into the sea of business—here you'll discover what qualities have ensured success for those who have set sail before you. You'll learn how to build on your strengths and how to navigate safely through the reefs and shoals that may lie ahead.

On the other hand, if your business career is in full sail, you'll learn how to enhance the level of excellence that you and your company continue to strive for and how to avoid the hidden dangers that lie in wait for the already successful. You'll feel rejuvenated, reinvigorated to set your sights on the stars and chart a course for new vistas as you rediscover what guided you on the successful passages you've already undertaken.

What's more, your guide in reaching for the stars and in becoming a star in your own right is someone who has made the voyage himself. Charles S. Lauer is publisher of *Modern Healthcare* and corporate vice president of Crain Communications in Chicago. His commitment to excellence and client/customer service is widely credited as being responsible for one of the great business success stories of recent years, the dramatic renaissance of *Modern Healthcare.*

That commitment to excellence accounts for the many prestigious awards Chuck has received, including Ohio State University's Distinguished Award for Leadership and Service, the American College of Healthcare Executives' Honorary Fellowship, and the American Institute of Architects' Presidential Recognition Award (which he was just the fourth person in forty-nine years to receive).

Chuck is a practical, successful businessman who knows the nuts and bolts of how to turn out a superb product that delights both client and customer and still turns a healthy profit.

But Chuck also has that rare ability to translate his insights into accessible, clear language that strikes a resonant chord in his listeners. That's why he has become one of the most sought-after speakers in all of American business. A typical month might see Chuck delivering eight speeches to business groups ranging from health care executives to the employees of a corporation such as Konica and to university students.

These communication skills also explain why Chuck's weekly "Publisher's Letter" column in *Modern Healthcare* is attentively read by business leaders nationwide. Those columns, along with excerpts from some of his speeches, have been revised and collected into this volume.

Even if you're not familiar with Chuck's column, you'll soon feel as if you've known him for years. His easy, familiar style is reminiscent of a conversation among friends gathered for a pleasant evening together, rather than the kind of dry reading that parches so many of today's soon-to-be-dusty business tomes.

Nestled in an easy informality that welcomes you as a partner in an ongoing dialogue, some stirring truths await you. Fresh insights into how to cope with the dizzying changes of business in the '90s stand side by side with reiterations of old-fashioned values seen afresh. Chuck continues to believe in the values that made America great—honesty, hard work, courage, loyalty, and perseverance—and isn't afraid to voice them at a time when much of the nation seems to have forgotten their importance.

One thing you won't find in *Reach for the Stars*, though, is a cold lecture. As far from holier-than-thou as you can get, Chuck imparts what he has learned by recalling his own mistakes. What he has learned from those mistakes and through studying the successes and failures of others he passes on to us. He's traveling the same road with us, pointing toward the same destination.

At the start of his poem *Song of Myself*, Walt Whitman promises his readers that

> You shall no longer take things at second or third hand, nor look
>   through the eyes of the dead, nor feed on the spectres in books,
> You shall not look through my eyes either, nor take things from
>   me,
> You shall listen to all sides and filter them from your self.

In the poem's concluding lines, Whitman extends his hand to those readers who haven't followed him, assuring them that

> Failing to fetch me at first keep encouraged,
> Missing me one place search another,
> I stop somewhere waiting for you.

Like Walt Whitman, Chuck Lauer treads the path alongside us, offering encouragement and inspiration. A genial guide with precious information and his own point of view, he puts his arm around his readers and helps them see for themselves. And like Walt Whitman, he believes in the goodness of the human spirit and the infinite possibilities of what that spirit can accomplish if we tap into its energy.

Chuck Lauer waits for you in these pages, ready to help you discover how to reach the stars. The first section, "Qualities for personal success," focuses on the traits necessary for success in any aspect of business—or, for that matter, life. Not specific to any particular job or industry, these are the talents and skills vital to high quality both as a worker and as a human being. "Inner qualities," the next section, urges us to assess our own inner resources and outlines the essential personal characteristics needed for success. It encourages us to be self-centered in the best sense: not by being selfish, but by being willing to examine our self—the core of our being—and to cultivate what we find.

Of course, that inner self can be tested by the hardships of everyday life. In "Coping with stress and disappointment in the business world," Chuck explores the ways the business world can extend deep into the heart of our lives. He offers valuable suggestions for coping with problems such as being laid off or suffering from too much stress.

How the world treats us affects how we treat the world in return. "How you treat others" moves us back toward the world, explaining how our marshaling of all that's inside—from our greatest talents to our deepest disappointments—can spell success. Here Chuck connects personal characteristics such as humility and decency with excellence in business.

Like the parts that follow, "Qualities for personal success" concludes with three remarkable profiles in success.

In the next major section, "Principles of success in action," Chuck helps us see how these qualities apply in the real world of competitive business. Starting at the top, he explores how leaders help to set a company's tone and philosophy ("Making your organization shine"). He then considers the point of contact with the customer ("Reaching the customer") and how to maintain that relationship once it's established ("Keeping the customer"). This development dictates the three specific areas explored in detail: success in management and leadership; success in sales and marketing; success in customer service.

Just as the opening section began with an exploration of the qualities necessary for personal success, each of these parts begins by examining the qualities necessary for success in that particular area (look for the ⚙ icon). Each of these parts also provides illustrations of potential stumbling blocks and practical strategies for overcoming them (indicated by the ⚡ icon). And each part concludes with three profiles in success (marked ♟)—portraits of people or companies that exemplify excellence in their fields.

These profiles offer worthy models for imitation and should give you an idea or two to try out on your own. Each part also offers one extended piece—"Lauer at length" (look for the ✍ icon)—in which Chuck spreads his wings beyond the usual length of his columns, lifts us up to soar with him, and surveys a particular subject from a wide view.

The closing section, "And then some...," adds a little extra to what the previous sections have said. And that, in a way, encapsulates the essence of Chuck Lauer's philosophy. He believes in always giving a little extra, whether it's to the customer, to your employees, or to your family. Giving your best...and then some—that's how one achieves true excellence, how one transcends reaching for the crumbs that others leave and ascends to the level of reaching for the stars.

At Williams College in Williamstown, Massachusetts, the following words are inscribed on the Hopkins Memorial Steps:

> Climb high
> Climb far
> Your goal the sky
> Your aim the star.

Chuck Lauer believes that we each have it in our power to fulfill our loftiest dreams. In this book, he charts our flight path.

Each of the items in this collection illuminates an area of business excellence. Gaze upon them at leisure. Jump from one to another if you wish, scanning at random. Or canvass the entirety from cover to cover. Together, they form a constellation of stellar advice, which can open up a universe of possibilities for you to aspire to—and attain—as you pursue your own mission and goals.

And somewhere within the galaxy of these pages, you might find a glimmering of the star you already are...and a way to make that star shine brighter than ever before.

Qualities for personal success

"Give every minute of your being 100 percent. Don't wait for things to happen to you. Go out and make things happen.... If you're enthusiastic and positive, people will beat a path to your door."

*S*UCCESS *is often understood to mean achievement in work—how high we climb the career
ladder. But such a definition falls short. For
success includes all of life. And far more than what
we do, it describes what we are.*

*A successful person is not just productive
but positive—not just a go-getter but a giver.
A successful person seeks excellence not only
in the workplace but in social, emotional,
intellectual, physical, and spiritual dimensions
as well.*

*For a successful person, nothing ranks higher
than possessing a personal character that reflects
time-tested virtues and values: honesty, resiliency,
perseverance, kindness, and the full slate of other
essential traits.*

Inner qualities

1
Simple strategies for success

THERE ARE A LOT of variables in success. I'm often asked what advice I would give to anybody embarking on a career regarding what it takes to get noticed. What is it that makes an individual stand out in any organization? A lot of it is basic common sense, but sometimes we overlook the simplest things in our quest for complex strategies for personal success.

First, there's enthusiasm. That will get you past all kinds of obstacles. People who are enthusiastic and positive create excitement in others. That means they have the first prerequisite for leadership. Enthusiasm, by the way, is one trait that can't be taught. It has to come from the heart. I know individuals who hold what some would call menial jobs, but they do their work with such fervor that you can't help but admire them. Think about the people you like to be around and you'll realize the importance of enthusiasm and positive thinking.

Next is loyalty—loyalty to yourself and to your organization. That trait stands right out and is one of the most important signs managers look for in employees. It's kind of chic these days to question the value of loyalty in light of all the downsizing and reengineering taking place—yet it's still important if you want to go places. Leaders are constantly looking for people they can count on.

Then there's the ability to communicate. Learn to write clearly and succinctly. Write simple, straightforward memos only one or two paragraphs long. Anything longer probably won't get read. Learn to respect other people's time.

Reading is a must as well. Read everything you can find about your industry. Know the latest fads and trends. Throw in the *Wall Street Journal* and the *New York Times*, and you'll be a star. Remember, knowledge is power.

4

Whether you're just starting out or you've been around a while, always be willing to do anything asked of you. Don't let false pride get in your way. Display a spirit of cooperation and be ready to jump in and do whatever needs to be done. There are too many prima donnas around these days who believe honest work is beneath them. Those people aren't going anywhere. And don't gossip about others or whine about your lot in life. It turns everybody off—including the boss.

Of course, getting along with your superiors helps. Never be adversarial with the boss. That's a sure way to short-circuit your career. I know a lot of bosses can act like jerks, but learning how to work with a difficult superior can offer some valuable lessons. Try to make the best of it.

The world is filled with gifted individuals who haven't gone anywhere with their careers because they haven't practiced the fundamentals. You can have a degree from the finest school in the country, but if you aren't enthusiastic, can't get along with your bosses, and aren't willing to give every day your best effort, you're destined for failure.

Finally, always keep your word. If you make a promise, honor that commitment. Never compromise your integrity. Believe me, others will notice.

2

The power of positive thinking lives on

MOST OF US WOULD AGREE that positive thinking is essential to a productive and successful life. Negative thinking leads to cynicism and failure, while a hopeful outlook and can-do attitude make many things possible.

I don't know about you, but I'm attracted to people who are enthusiastic and positive about life. They inspire and invigorate me with their willingness to focus on the bright side of things. I don't like complainers and whiners, because they take the joy out of living. Positive individuals think the world is their oyster and usually go out and prove it. To me, positive thinking is essential, so I was saddened back in 1993 to hear about the death of Dr. Norman Vincent Peale at the age of ninety-five.

Some people may not know about Dr. Peale, but back in the early '50s and through the '60s, '70s, and even into the '80s, he was considered by many as the one who made positive thinking so much a part of people's lives.

His influence is still apparent in many of today's motivational and inspirational books, seminars, and speeches. Dr. Peale's book *The Power of Positive Thinking* (Prentice Hall, 1952) probably started it all. He was courted by presidents and corporate executives who were attracted by his simple formula for success. Dr. Peale believed that a positive state of mind could be induced with simple prayer, which in turn could produce spiritual and material success.

In retrospect, Norman Vincent Peale's simple formula came along at the right time. The country was still recovering from the Great Depression and World War II, and everyone was seeking a basic plan to enjoy life and find success. Along came Dr. Peale's book, and the rest is history.

In his lifetime, Dr. Peale wrote forty-one books and was considered one of the great preachers of our time. He not only gave sermons but also wrote newspaper columns and made radio broadcasts, making him known worldwide for his positive outlook on life.

But there's an interesting twist to all of this. In an interview, Dr. Peale admitted that many of his best sermons had been directed at himself because he was either depressed or foundering in his beliefs.

During his career, Dr. Peale had plenty of critics, many of them in the clergy, who accused him of oversimplifying religion. But to this criticism Dr. Peale had a frank response. In an interview in 1978, he had this to say: "Many ministers said my book *[The Power of Positive Thinking]* was oversimplified and wasn't couched in the correct ecclesiastical language. That was true.

It was written in simple language because I was trying to reach people who were not in the church."

Dr. Peale's roots were in the Midwest. He was born in Bowersville, Ohio, in 1898. His father, a former physician, was a Methodist minister serving several congregations in southern Ohio. Dr. Peale made his decision to become a minister after he heard his father giving a sermon asking for sinners to come forth and be saved. According to the story, the town drunkard responded to the call by coming forward, kneeling at the altar and praying for forgiveness. They say the man never took another drink after that.

During his first summer back home while attending the Boston University School of Theology, the young Norman Vincent Peale was asked to give a sermon for an ailing pastor. He agreed, writing the sermon in the best divinity-school language he knew. He then showed his work to his father, who told him: "My advice would be to take it out back and burn it." His father then explained that the best way to the human heart is through simplicity.

From that advice we can all learn a lesson. Keep things simple in writing, speaking, and living. Better still, always put a big dose of positive thinking into everything you do. It makes all the difference in the world.

3
It's how you play the game

 WHAT DO YOU THINK OF when you hear the term *sportsmanship*? We admire individuals who display fair play in their professional and personal lives, who play by the rules, who enjoy being part of a team and winning as a team.

They usually believe in honor, truthfulness, and honesty. They don't like cheating or cheaters and, if they discover someone breaking the rules, they let that person know about it. When they win, they do so gracefully; when they lose, they show they are good sports by congratulating the winner. That's the kind of attitude that should be an integral part of our lives. But today, the term *sportsmanship* is seldom heard, while winning no matter what has almost become a creed. It's wrong, and it's perverting our impressionable youth.

Don't get me wrong. I like winning, and I'm sure you do too. But a victory based on cheating or vanquishing an opponent is a hollow one. That's not what sports are all about. However, we've managed to turn every major sport into a virtual circus, from the professional level down to the little leagues. We've lost something precious, and so have our kids.

I've gone to "squirt" hockey games for children ages eight to ten and have witnessed shocking behavior by parents in the stands. They should be setting an example for their kids, not simply about winning and losing but about the sheer joy of participating in a team sport and having fun playing a game. Sports should be about joy and fun and competition—those are the lessons of sports, and that's why children should participate in them. How someone handles losing is just as important as how someone behaves after winning.

I've followed sports all my life, as well as participating in them. I've seen more displays of character and honor by those who have lost than by those who have triumphed. It means something—it shows what people are made of and whether or not they can recover after suffering a heartbreaking defeat.

Sadly, a lot of children who participate in sports—or, for that matter, play chess or compete in the classroom—believe they are losers if they don't win all the time. The irony is that giving your best is what really counts. Too many people believe they're losers because they didn't make the varsity team, didn't get accepted into their first-choice college, or didn't accomplish something else they hoped to.

But there should be more emphasis on one's civil deportment

on a day-to-day basis; we should rejoice over those who go out of their way to be good teammates and colleagues and give every day their best.

Sports should teach stamina, an ability to lose with honor, and a willingness to be a decent, fair-minded person. Sportsmanship is synonymous with life's basic lessons. It's learning to live with others in peace and treating others fairly. So get on the field, play the game, and give every play your all. Most of the time, if you do that, you'll win. But if you lose, remember that the important thing is that you had the courage to play the game.

Above all, it's *how* you play the game.

4
Shine like a star

NO MATTER WHAT PROFESSION you're in, you simply have to know how to read and write. That sounds so simple, doesn't it? After all, reading and writing are supposedly the fundamentals of a good education. At least that's what you've always believed, and I still do. If people can't express themselves verbally or in writing, how are they going to communicate with their bosses, their customers, or their mates? It's that essential, but, unfortunately, too many individuals today simply haven't been drilled in these basics.

Talk to college professors or corporate recruiters and they'll tell you that a lot of kids today simply can't communicate properly. To bring this premise full circle, the reason they can't is that in order to be able to write effectively and to speak with authority, a person first has to read. That's where it all begins.

How many of us are reading as much as we should? Think about it. Are you reading everything you should about your profession? Do you enjoy reading books and novels that enhance your understanding of new concepts and ideas? I know individuals in industry who make jokes about how little they read. But then they make decisions based on uninformed and outmoded thinking that in the end probably will lead to failure and in many cases will cost their companies money.

Why aren't people reading? They're just too busy. Studies tell us that people are working longer hours and are actually more productive, but the time they have for other pursuits is getting shorter and shorter. That, of course, includes time for reading.

Then there's TV. With cable and VCRs, there are all sorts of alternatives to cuddling up with that book or magazine. TV doesn't require too much effort. Just push the button to change the channel. Reading takes effort and involves gray matter. Unfortunately, the easy way out usually wins.

Look around the country and the situation becomes even more depressing. We've lost newspapers in many major marketing areas—not just ordinary papers, but great ones as well. That's not only because of commuting and television but because the number of readers continues to decline.

Presidential elections are a classic example of what's happening. How many people do you believe are able to make sound judgments on what each candidate stands for based on in-depth reading of the issues? Not many, I bet. Too frequently our command of the issues is based on what we see on *Larry King Live* and other TV talk shows.

My point is this: If you can read well and write well, you'll stand out. You'll be able to communicate better, whether it's to sell a product or to ask for a raise or promotion. The ability to read proficiently enables you to verbalize things better and gives substance and clarity to what you say, because it's based on knowledge.

So there they are, the three essentials: reading, writing, and speaking. Reading is hard work, so you have to make an effort and set aside some time in your busy day. Writing is one of the most difficult disciplines known to man. You have to practice it over and over. You probably won't get it right the first time, but when you do, you'll feel great about it. Then there's speaking. When it comes to verbalizing something, it always comes easier if you've read about the issues. After all, understanding gives you confidence.

Nothing earthshaking here, just a simple approach to success. Reading opens the door to life's adventure; writing gives you the ability to convey ideas; the ability to speak makes you an even more effective communicator. It all takes work, but if you make the effort, you'll shine just like the star you should be.

5

How Perseverance beat a path to the door of Success

THEY'RE THREE QUITE DIFFERENT personalities. Three individuals who have left indelible marks on the American scene. Three individuals who kept going even though the doom-and-gloomers did everything they could to discourage them. One majored in making hamburgers, one was a songwriter, and the other is a salesman. What do they have in common? Call it intestinal fortitude or just plain gumption—they persevered.

Ray Kroc formed McDonald's. He had a dream, which was to make good hamburgers and then franchise hamburger restaurants all over the country. Talk about a success story. A lot of people thought he was nuts and a little eccentric, but show me an entrepreneur who isn't a little bit different from the rest of us. In Howard E. Ferguson's book *The Edge* (Getting the Edge Co.), the late Mr. Kroc explained his formula for success: "I am convinced that to be a success in business, you must be first, you must be daring, and you must be different."

But there was something else he believed in: the power of

perseverance. As he put it, "Nothing in the world can take the place of persistence. Talent will not; nothing is more common than unsuccessful men with talent. Genius will not; unrewarded genius is almost a proverb. Education alone will not; the world is full of educated derelicts. Persistence and determination alone are omnipotent." Ray Kroc was a legend in his own time.

Then there's Jule Styne, the late songwriter. Over seven decades he wrote fifteen hundred songs and was awarded an Oscar and a Tony. He was really the last link to the great American songwriters such as Irving Berlin, Cole Porter, George Gershwin, Jerome Kern, and Richard Rodgers. All of them honed their craft during the '20s and '30s on Broadway. Mr. Styne gave Barbra Streisand and Carol Channing their signature songs. In the case of Ms. Streisand, it was "People," and for Ms. Channing, it was "Diamonds Are a Girl's Best Friend." Some of his other songs are "Make Someone Happy," "It's Been a Long, Long Time," and "The Party's Over."

Mr. Styne got an early start in the music business, making his debut as a child pianist with the Chicago Symphony Orchestra. Along the way, however, he was told his hands were too small for him to be a concert pianist. So he turned to jazz and went on to jam with the likes of Louis Armstrong, Bix Beiderbecke, and Benny Goodman, among others. He didn't give up; he just changed course. He, too, was a legend in his own time.

Then there's Donald A. Macdonald, vice chairman emeritus of Dow Jones and Co. He's probably best known for setting the standards and business strategies of the modern *Wall Street Journal*. In his book *Arrows in Your Quiver* (Dow Jones and Co., 1994) he talks about his philosophy of selling and living. But it's his advice to those just starting their careers that stands out: "There are surely very good people working alongside of you. There are people who are probably smarter than you. There are people who can sell better than you. But, what you tend to forget is that all these people do not necessarily want to take on additional responsibility. More and more, year after year, as the jobs grow larger or as the challenges become more difficult, fewer people truly want them."

That challenge spells opportunity. In short, Mr. Macdonald is reminding us that hard work always pays. Mr. Macdonald is a member of the Advertising Hall of Fame and has received a host of other honors and titles. He's another legend in his own time.

There's no great intellectual discourse here, just plain old common sense. Things like hard work, believing in oneself, and determination are all part of the biographies of successful people. It's all spelled out in the lives of Kroc, Styne, and Macdonald. When others would have given up, they stuck it out.

6
The qualities employers look for

ONE OF THE MOST important attributes that employers look for when hiring is an applicant's ability to get along with other people. Too often the ability to work well with others is overlooked because the interviewer is more concerned about the person's education, job skills, and his or her appearance. I would think all of us agree that education, experience, and appearance are important factors, but a recent study suggests that many employers feel other factors are even more important.

The editors of *Communication Briefings*, a newsletter I read, asked four hundred subscribers to identify the traits they felt were most important to the success of a person's career. The findings were somewhat surprising, although they really shouldn't be. Some 84 percent of the respondents cited interpersonal skills, including good manners and the ability to get along well with others; 79 percent said the ability to write well was crucial; and 68 percent said they look for good speaking ability.

Surprisingly, only 40 percent rated educational background and work experience high in the traits they sought. Personal appearance was dead last, with only 18 percent saying it's vital to someone's career.

So what does this all mean? Well, foremost, it means that businesses are looking for people who not only get the job done but can make things happen with a spirit of teamwork and cooperation. That's so essential in today's competitive climate. Mavericks and prima donnas are fine under certain circumstances, but in most business situations employers need people who want to work well with others and who don't mind subjugating their egos to the common cause of a project or sale. All it takes is one person to screw things up for everyone.

A good analogy can be drawn with sports, because if one individual on a team goes his or her own way, the team isn't going to succeed. That in turn brings about low morale; soon losing becomes a habit. Such a cycle spells disaster for any organization.

As far as writing skills are concerned, I can't stress that ability enough. With the growth of electronic communication through such devices as personal computers and fax machines, the ability to write concisely is growing even more important. Too many people don't examine their writing abilities critically enough—and they should. Be humble enough to ask a colleague or anyone else you know who will give you a truthful answer about your writing. If you have a problem, there are all sorts of books and courses available to help you improve your skills. Sure, it will take time and discipline, but eventually it will help your career.

The ability to speak well is also essential for any individual who wants to achieve success. And it's so easy to learn if you're willing to practice. But again, it will take time.

Yes, appearance is important, especially in sales, where you always want to present a professional image. But if you can't articulate what you want other people to do or what your product is all about, you aren't going to have much luck. I've interviewed some very attractive people seeking sales jobs, but when it came to telling me about themselves and their strengths, some began to stammer and became so tongue-tied that I knew they would be ineffective. It's sad, because being able to sell yourself with words is the gist and genius of sales.

I'd like to add three traits that I always name when asked what I look for in hiring sound performers. The traits are enthusiasm, character, and perseverance.

Genuine enthusiasm is the basic ingredient that determines how an individual will approach his or her job. It's the crucial element, because without enthusiasm a lot of other things won't fall into line. It's a contagious condition, so if you're lucky enough to be around truly enthusiastic individuals, you're bound to be affected. Most people are naturally attracted to others who display enthusiasm.

When I'm interviewing someone, I try to determine immediately that person's enthusiasm level. Does this person simply want a job in order to earn a paycheck, or does he or she really want to make a commitment and continually give more than just enough to get by? With the right questions, it's really not too hard to determine. Often when someone is genuinely enthusiastic, I don't have to ask any questions at all because that level of enthusiasm will be so evident.

And then I always look for basic character. Do the applicants believe in themselves? Do they have a set of principles? What do they want to do with their careers? How do they motivate themselves? Are they givers or takers? The answers to these kinds of questions can reveal how people will react under pressure or how they will treat their colleagues. Character is a tough element to measure, but it's so essential. It's important in building a solid team of people who will represent a company well.

Finally there's steadfastness. Sometimes it's referred to as persistence. By this I mean the ability to handle adversity and rejection, to look at a situation that needs fixing and without coaching just go ahead and handle it. This takes a person who will charge ahead regardless of the obstacles and make something positive happen.

So just for the fun of it, why don't you rate yourself on your people skills, writing skills, and speaking skills? Rate yourself on your enthusiasm, character, and perseverance. We can all work on our weaknesses. If you're honest with yourself, you might find you have some work to do in one or two areas or maybe even all of them. But if you have the intestinal fortitude to grade yourself honestly, you might just help yourself to achieve greater success.

7

The wisdom of poetry

I WAS TALKING to one of my colleagues the other day, and somehow our conversation got around to poetry. She told me she really didn't have the time anymore to read anything but business things—trade journals, the *Wall Street Journal*, reports, and other information pertaining to her job. As far as poetry was concerned, she simply hadn't read much of it since high school. That got me to thinking that she probably wasn't much different from many of us whose schedules are often busier than we'd like.

So when I got home that night I looked through some books I had read in high school and college, and the one I finally chose to spend some time with was *Selections From Browning* (Ginn and Co., 1906), edited by Robert Morss Lovett of the University of Chicago. Robert Browning is, of course, considered one of the greatest English poets—along with the Romantic poets from the late eighteenth and early nineteenth century, such as Wordsworth, Coleridge, Byron, Keats, Shelley, and Scott. During that era, men were trying to escape the limited opportunities for freedom of expression. Mr. Browning was more of a realist, and with the waning of the Romantic movement he chose to reflect his percep-tions of living in the Victorian era. Above all, he was filled with enthusiasm for life and people. These feelings are reflected in his poetry. To this day, many of his messages have applications in business or any other pursuit.

Mr. Browning believed that men and women were being tested continually by the tribulations of everyday living, but he felt that challenge was the beauty of life. He also felt deeply that life was not a perfect social organization and that success came in many forms and under many circumstances. As a matter of fact, he believed that one of the biggest sins anyone could commit was simply not to accept challenge and therefore not to grapple with all the disappointments and successes that challenge brings.

Something else he disdained was reaching a goal too easily and feeling satisfied with that accomplishment. In his poem "Andrea del Sarto," the speaker, an artist named Andrea del Sarto, tells us, "A man's reach should exceed his grasp." In other words, challenge yourself; don't sit still. Give life a shake. In "Rabbi Ben Ezra," the poem's speaker tells us,

> Then, welcome each rebuff
> That turns earth's smoothness rough,
> Each sting that bids nor sit nor stand but go!

Browning believed that activity, energy, and vitality could overcome any obstacle.

Now, I know English literature isn't necessarily where one is going to learn to swim with the sharks or where one will learn new and shrewd negotiating methods, but I do believe that we sometimes forget the insights and practical lessons that poetry and great literature can offer us. Rich works surround us, but they usually lie dormant. When I go back from time to time and read Emerson, Thoreau, Whitman, and Frost, I am immensely refreshed and in many ways reborn. Their works are original and basic. Their wisdom will go down through the ages, yet too many of us are so busy with "business things" that we miss the riches of literature.

Maybe another line from "Andrea del Sarto" is applicable here: "So free we seem, so fettered fast we are!" It just may be that we're looking for inspiration and guidance concerning our careers and our lives in all the wrong places. A poem might not be a bad place to start.

17

8
Battling the gremlins
of disorganization and ego

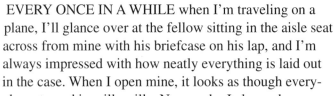

EVERY ONCE IN A WHILE when I'm traveling on a plane, I'll glance over at the fellow sitting in the aisle seat across from mine with his briefcase on his lap, and I'm always impressed with how neatly everything is laid out in the case. When I open mine, it looks as though everything has been tossed in willy-nilly. No wonder I always have a tough time finding this or that report I was planning to read during the flight. There just never seems to be enough time in a day, so when it's time to catch a plane, I usually grab everything in sight that I think I'll need, throw it into my briefcase, and dash out. I guess that would explain my problem.

Then there's parking at the airport. I don't know how many times I've come back from a trip and not been able to find my car. I'll say to myself that I know I parked it on the fourth level, but somehow when I'm finally able to track it down, it's been mysteriously moved to the sixth level. One time I actually reported my car stolen to security at O'Hare Airport in Chicago, but the individual I talked to was kind enough to go out with me for one more look before we filled out the paperwork. Sure enough, we found it, but it was another case of gremlins moving my car.

My secretary is extremely cautious when she deals with me concerning any kind of document she deems important. She'll usually show me the document but continue to hold on to it with one hand until I can decide whether we should make additional copies. Unfortunately, it seems the more important something is, the easier it is for me to misplace it. In some cases, it only takes a matter of seconds before a paper my secretary has given me

18

somehow disappears. I've even accused colleagues of removing things from my desk.

Speaking of my desk, when I'm in action during the day, the top of my desk looks like someone came in and literally dumped a bunch of papers and other things on it. Hidden somewhere in the piles and under the empty coffee cups are the reports and memos I read and prepare during the course of my working day. I have a friend in New York in the same business, and it always irks me when I walk into his office and there's virtually nothing on his desk. And usually when I interrupt him, he's calmly sitting there reading the *New York Times.* On top of that, he never seems to have a hair out of place and, as a rule, is impeccably dressed. I don't know how he does it.

I bring all this up because someone complimented me the other day by telling me how organized he thought I was. I chortled. He was taken aback when I said I didn't think I was any more organized than the next person and offered some examples. But there are people who are quite neurotic about these things and take themselves very seriously about being so organized. They actually think it's a sign of weakness to show disorganization or any other human frailty, and they'll go to all sorts of extremes to show just how perfect and together they are.

Sadly, they won't even admit that they make mistakes. Apparently, it's an ego thing with some people, and it can be demoralizing and debilitating for colleagues, especially if the person in question is the boss. Saying words such as *I'm sorry, I made a mistake,* or *That was my fault,* saves a lot of time and heartache. It also shows humility and candor, which in turn make other individuals feel better. It bothers me when individuals pretend to be something they're not, because they're not being honest with themselves or with others.

Showing people respect is part of the process too. Being a decent human being is a sign of strength.

Coping with stress
and disappointment
in the business world

9
Take the time to relieve stress

SOMEDAY, MAYBE, enlightened companies and even graduate schools of business will offer courses on how to handle stress. On-the-job stress touches us all—some more than others—because we put ourselves under tremendous pressure to do the best job possible at whatever we're doing.

Add travel into the equation and it gets even more complicated. There are all kinds of other things you can throw into the pot, including internal politics, troubles at home, and unrealistic deadlines set by superiors. All these tend to be cumulative and can take a toll on a person's mental and physical health. We've all been through it or are going through it.

Job stress is probably one of the most misunderstood phenomena in American business. I've read articles that suggest some stress in the workplace is positive and helps certain employees to excel, but I've also read other articles that deliver warnings about how the negative impact of stress can cripple otherwise talented and hard-driving individuals.

Heart attacks, alcoholism, and divorce are just a few of the consequences that can result when stress enters one's life. In many cases stress can be devastating, even fatal. Stories about the effects of stress are familiar to all of us. Good friends of mine have died from heart attacks brought on by too much travel and booze. And I'm sure every one of us has read the obituary of some forty-five- to fifty-year-old executive who was on a trip somewhere and suddenly died of a heart attack. A wife and kids are usually left behind.

Stress has become such a major problem in business that it costs industry in the United States about $200 billion annually, according to a 1993 report by the International Labor Organization, an arm of the United Nations. I learned a lot about the cost of stress

21

from an article written that same year by Frank Grazian, then executive editor of *Communication Briefings*, a newsletter written for busy executives. In the article I read, Mr. Grazian discussed the ILO report, titled "Job Stress: The Twentieth Century Disease."

According to the report, stress-related injury claims on the job climbed from 5 percent of all occupational disease claims in 1980 to 15 percent a decade later. The $200 billion figure was based on "compensation claims, reduced productivity, absenteeism, added health insurance costs and direct medical expenses for related diseases such as ulcers, high blood pressure and heart attacks."

One major cause of stress, the report said, is the constant monitoring of employees—everything from checking up on how quickly they perform a task to the frequency and length of their breaks. And although companies are increasingly contributing to the causes of stress, they aren't doing much to help their employees deal with it.

Mr. Grazian offers some advice to companies to help their employees cope. He starts out by stating that employee helplessness and uncertainty are two major causes of stress. Companies can eliminate the problem by encouraging employees to do their best and making sure they know they're trusted. Also, companies must give employees regular playback on how well they're doing their jobs. In other words, let people know how much they're valued.

Many companies are now beginning to recognize how important it is to monitor their people to make sure they're keeping everything in balance. That's a good start, but there's still a long way to go. It's great to be a high achiever, but success at the expense of your health and family is too high a price to pay.

Antidotes to stress include exercise, good nutrition, vacations, sleep, and lots of laughter. We all know what to do, but I keep hearing the same excuse over and over: "I just don't have time." Well, maybe now's the time to take the time. Furthermore, I maintain that those who do get their lives in order are more effective, no matter what their position. They think more clearly and rationally, which usually spells success.

A friend and I had breakfast a while back. He mentioned to me that he had taken a sabbatical from his frequent business travel. He put it this way: "I used to travel 80 percent of the time, but now I'm traveling about 10 percent. It has made all the difference in the world." This is a highly placed executive with a *Fortune* 500 company. While this fellow loves a good challenge, he explained what made him realize some changes were in order: "My family was suffering, and I couldn't let that go on."

He also began experiencing gastrointestinal problems. On top of that, he told me he was fatigued all the time. "When I would get home, I simply wanted to rest so much I wasn't much fun to anyone. That's why I cut back on the travel and let my people do more of it. Funny as it may seem, things seem to be running more smoothly." In other words, he finally learned to delegate.

In the article I mentioned, Mr. Grazian suggests ways we can deal with stress better. More often than not, he says, stress is based on a perception of something threatening. Try to change that perception by stepping back and asking yourself how you can change the situation. There must be something in the situation you can control. Concentrate on achieving that control—and do it.

Another suggestion is to develop a commitment to your job. In other words, think of your job as a mission. Determine what's unique about your job. This gives you a better perspective so you can react to your own pressures.

Develop additional job skills. Take courses, read books, seek out the advice of experts in your field. Learn as much as you can about your work. When you do, you'll feel a lot more confident about your job, which should help reduce the stress load. Also, try to avoid being a perfectionist. Just do the best you can do.

Gain control of as many aspects of your life as you can. If work isn't going so well, there may be things on the home front that can give you a better sense of accomplishment and build up your self-esteem. This is important for all of us.

Finally, remember that exercise helps relieve stress, too, along with a big dose of laughter.

Stress is hard to avoid, especially in the world we live in today. No doubt about it, a certain amount of stress is good for us. It keeps us on our toes and helps us excel. But too much can be dangerous, even deadly. That's where all of us have to be careful.

Life is filled with difficult situations, but if we are to have long, healthy lives and successful careers, learning to cope with stress is essential.

10
Follow that dream

ALL OF US, at one time or another, have had to endure the put-down. I'm referring to when people are told that they just don't have the right stuff to make it, either in life or in a particular profession. It can be very discouraging, and if the recipients of this kind of doom-and-gloom prophecy aren't focused and don't have a healthy level of self-esteem, they sometimes simply give up. They walk away and tell themselves they just don't have it. But there will always be that nagging question in the back of their minds—could I have done it?

Put-downs happen all the time. Bosses do it, coaches do it, teachers do it. There's no end to the number of people who put others down, intentionally or unintentionally. But here's a simple piece of advice: Don't ever let it happen to you.

In many cases, individuals who put others down are bullies. They don't feel good about themselves, so their only defense for their own inadequacies is to make others feel bad about themselves. You see it and hear it all the time: "You'll never amount to much, because you're lazy," or "Nobody can make that sale, especially you." Or this one: "You'll never make the team. You aren't big enough." People who say such things are trying to take away others' dreams. But just remember that those who would do this are the real losers.

History books and everyday life are filled with stories about people who have overcome incredible odds to fulfill their dreams.

Some people have such unrelenting drive that they conquer all sorts of physical handicaps that would discourage the average human being.

One of the anecdotes I use when I speak to various groups has to do with Fred Astaire. Back in 1935, the great dancer had his first screen test. At the conclusion of the test, the person in charge told him: "Mr. Astaire, I'm sorry to tell you that you are not very good at acting. Your singing voice is at best mediocre, and you do not dance well." Imagine that. If Fred Astaire had followed that person's advice and given up, we all would have missed the genius and warmth of his many talents.

There are so many stories like that. For instance, there's the lesson of one Winston Churchill, who finished last upon graduation from the British equivalent of high school. None of his teachers thought he was headed anywhere.

Aside from the hard knocks of life, no test can measure what is in a person's heart. Never let others tell you what you can or cannot accomplish. If you believe in yourself and have the energy and courage, anything is possible.

There are people who will criticize you, and there are those who will make fun of you, but there are also others who will support you and encourage you to reach for new heights. Listen to them, but most important, listen to your heart. Make your dreams come true. You know yourself best; no one else can really know what you're capable of accomplishing.

11
Go for the gold!

ONE OF MY BASIC THEMES, when I speak to various groups, is that one should never, but never, give up, no matter what the odds.

Adversity and defeat are tough things to handle, but then so is success. Yet the difference is like night and day. Many people just don't like to go for the gold, because it truly frightens them. Still others like the security of predictability; taking a chance seems foolhardy to them. Consequently, to my way of thinking, they miss so much in life.

In a speech to the Washington Touchdown Club in 1960, John F. Kennedy spoke these words: "In life, the credit goes not to the critic that stands on the sidelines and points out when the strong man stumbles. The real credit in life goes to the man in the arena whose face gets marred by sweat and dust and mud, who knows great enthusiasm and great devotion, and learns to spend himself in a worthy cause. If he wins, he knows the thrill of high achievement. If he fails, he at least fails while daring greatness. His life will never be with those cold and timid souls who know neither victory nor defeat."

Those words energize me. They make me want to do better and work harder.

Some people worry too much about failure. They worry that they'll embarrass themselves or that others will make fun of them. But if you truly care and if you truly want to be successful, you have to believe in yourself. That takes intestinal fortitude—the willingness to make sacrifices and take hard knocks. After all, there are no guarantees in life, and there shouldn't be. That's the fun of living, as well as the heartache of living. Taking chances and striving to be better than average is what the pursuit of excellence is all about.

Losers sit on the sidelines and make fun of the doers. They can't stand to see someone else win, because it screws up their whole cynical attitude that hard work doesn't pay off.

Why do I bring all of this up? Maybe it's because I hear so many people who seem to believe the world owes them a living. Because they've done this or that, for some reason this country owes them employment. That's baloney, and that's arrogance.

Don't get me wrong. I've lost my job at one time or another in my career, so I know the desperation and insecurity that sets in. It isn't pretty. But my dad taught me never to give up and never to think the world owes me anything. His words have stuck with me through good times and bad, and they've never steered me wrong.

My dad also believed in this nation of ours. He believed in the opportunity that abounds out there for those who'll take a few risks and go for the gold. It's there, no question about it, but the rewards won't go to those who think the world is going to come to their door just because they went to a top school or they come from a nice family. Opportunity and rewards go to those who want to be on the playing field and who believe in giving 100 percent every day.

Put another way, winners make their own luck. They make things happen. They fail a lot, too, but they always get up again and again and get back into the game.

12
Volle est posse: Latin for "success"

MANY YEARS AGO, I attended a small, all-boys prep school in Hamilton, Ontario, Canada. It was patterned after English schools, and the headmaster was Philip Kilip, a tall Englishman who could put the fear of God into any student

with one glance. Now here was a man dedicated to academic
excellence as well as discipline. The name of the school was
Hillfield. I studied there during World War II. Many of the
students were young English kids whose parents had sent them to
Canada for safekeeping during the awful blitz the Germans were
applying to the British Isles in an attempt to break the English
will. But despite the constant bombing and the endless pressure
the Germans brought to bear against them, the British people
never broke. As a matter of fact, the attacks only strengthened
their indomitable spirit.

I bring all this up because I can remember so vividly my
training at Hillfield and the wonderful friends I made there. It was
a very disciplined environment. If a student stepped out of line, he
could get a strapping right in front of the entire class. Worse still,
if a student did something really awful, such as using profanity, he
was summoned to the headmaster's office, where he would be
caned. Strapping was simply a straight-razor strop applied to the
palm of the offender's hand five or six times. Caning was more
serious and more painful. The headmaster would apply a switch
cane two or three times to the offender's posterior. Unfortunately,
I suffered both punishments a number of times, and I still shudder
when I think of them.

The honor code was an essential component of student life at
Hillfield. Cheating just wasn't tolerated. And sports were important too. All the boys except those with serious health problems
were expected to participate in the various school sports. There
was always a big Games Day and a cross-country run in which all
the students participated. It was quite something, and there was
always plenty of esprit de corps among the students. Everyone
helped each other and everyone cared for the other guy. It was that
simple.

And the school's motto was something I'll always remember,
because it was so important then—and it still is today. It was
simply *volle est posse*, which loosely translated from Latin means,
"Where there is a will, there is a way." I always remember that
phrase when things aren't going so well or when I'm feeling
depressed. I look around and marvel at the individuals who've

persevered and have shown that if you really want to, you can do anything.

Put another way, don't listen to all the "grave dancers" who tell you why you can't do something or that things are so bad you won't even come close. What do they know? They don't know how big your heart is or how determined you are. There are all kinds of tests that can measure your intelligence quotient, but they can't measure your common sense quotient. And I've yet to see a test that can measure intestinal fortitude.

I'm tired of people making excuses for why they can't do better. I simply tell those people to just swing into action and make things happen. Don't dwell on the negative. Instead, accentuate the positive and work harder. That's perseverance.

Years ago, a buddy of mine told me that he had only a grade-school education, but over the years he learned how to compensate for his limited formal schooling. How did he do it? He told me that if you can't outthink the next guy, you can always outwork him. And that's what he's done all of his life. In doing so, he made the publishing company he headed one of the most successful in the country.

Too many people today are looking at the gloomy side of things. They're scared and insecure because they don't believe in themselves. They don't believe in the promise of America, and they're blind to the countless opportunities all around them. Don't sit still; go out and make things happen. Success is there if you want it badly enough, but it takes courage, honor, and sacrifice.

That's how you spell success.

13
How to cope with being fired

HEARTACHE. IT'S HARD to define and comes in all sizes and shapes, but when it hits, it can be devastating. There seems to be a lot of it going around right now, affecting some really good, solid people. I'm referring specifically to when people lose their jobs. It's tough.

Generally, those I have run into put a good face on the situation, but being fired or "let go" can be traumatic. Leaving a company or organization shouldn't be the end of the world, but some people who go through this sort of thing are so traumatized that they find it difficult to carry on. When it happens, things are never quite the same again. You don't really understand what you have until it's taken away from you. But if it does happen, don't despair. In the long run, you'll probably end up in a better job than the one you lost. Let me explain.

This whole subject came up when a good friend of mine told me he was being released from his job because his company was downsizing. He's middle-aged, very competent, and has plenty of drive, ambition, and discipline. I didn't think he would be out of work very long, but when I saw him, he had a bad case of "I'm feeling sorry for myself." That's OK, but only if it lasts for about five minutes.

For the record, I have been out of work a couple of times myself and know what goes on in one's mind—the despair, the isolation, the feeling of failure. The first time it happened to me was early in my career when my sales territory was combined with someone else's and I was the odd man out.

The second time I was released because, even though I had been given a promotion to the top sales job, I made the decision not to move my family to the West Coast. It was only a matter of

30

time before I had to go, and, of course, it didn't take long for that to happen.

My advice to my friend went along these lines: First, take some time to assess your situation. By that I mean not to make any decisions right away about what you're going to do. Don't forget, right after being fired you're probably not thinking too straight. Who would be after that kind of thing happens? Weigh your options and decide whether you really want to stay in the field you're in or whether there's something you've always dreamed of doing but just didn't have the time or opportunity to explore. Think things through.

No matter what the circumstances, leave the organization in a positive manner with a smile on your face. This is one of the most difficult things to do and takes great self-control, but in the long run it pays off. Don't forget that you will probably want to ask someone at the company you leave for a reference, and how you conduct yourself as you depart could make all the difference in the world.

One gentleman came to see me after he had been terminated, and the only thing he could talk about was how terribly his past employer had treated him. That doesn't sell. Don't knock your former employer. No matter how right you are or how grave the injustice done to you, it still sounds like sour grapes. Be positive and enthusiastic about who you are and what you can bring to the workplace. A positive attitude sells, and the person interviewing you can't help but be impressed.

Another piece of advice: Don't hold grudges and don't be bitter. Get on with your life, and work as hard as you can to find new employment. Work harder than you ever worked in your life. Make telephone calls early in the morning to the top executives. By early, I'm not talking about 9 in the morning; I'm talking about 6:30 or 7:30 when a lot of the bosses arrive. Remember, everyone is looking for self-starters and go-getters.

A number of business gurus believe that people really don't begin to mature until they've lost a couple jobs. These experts believe it gives a person more depth and sensitivity, and that's what companies look for today—people who care about others and can work in a team environment. Those aren't the only traits, of course, but they're high on the list of things employers look for when interviewing. So avoid feeling sorry for yourself, and don't sit around and mope. Get out and start looking right away. Network with your friends, former colleagues, and anybody else you can think of who might help in your job search.

But don't be shocked if a lot of people you thought were your friends suddenly go silent after you're fired. These types are what they call front-runners—people who are with you when everything's rosy but disappear fast when there are clouds on the horizon. On the other hand, you'll be pleasantly surprised by the number of people who surface and are genuinely concerned about your status. They are your real friends. You probably didn't know how much they cared, because you were too busy with your job. Don't ever take them for granted again.

Finding employment is tough, grinding work. That's when your perseverance will be tested. See as many people as you can. Talk to anyone who will listen. Don't let false pride get in your way. Be direct and honest when you are interviewed. Let them know how much you want the job and how hard you'll work if you're hired. Interviewers look for individuals who are hungry and willing to give that extra effort.

When you get an interview, forget about false pride and make a pitch for how hard-working you are and how much you really want the job. Many executives tell me that the people they interview often don't ask for the job. They apparently think that's too crass or beneath them. That's too bad, because with that kind of attitude they'll probably be out of work for quite some time.

For everyone who's out there laboring to leave the ranks of the jobless, I'll tell you this: If you have anything on the ball at all, you are going to do well. I'll even make a bet you'll land a job that not only pays better but also offers more opportunity to do what you do best. I talk to a lot of people, many of whom have been fired from previous jobs. But they all seem to be doing so much better today and exude a newfound confidence in their abilities.

One other point. Whenever you hear of someone you care about who is having a run of bad luck, let him or her know, somehow, that you care. A phone call, a note, or a visit can do wonders for that person's morale.

You'll get offers, plenty of them, but be choosy. Don't take the first thing that comes along. In the meantime, don't get down on yourself and feel guilty just because you've gotten the ax. Actually, you've gained invaluable insights into who you are and what you're capable of doing. And you'll be better off because of it.

Losing a job is never the end of the world. Although it's painful, you'll learn a lot about yourself and probably become a much better human being for what you've gone through.

Humility is a great teacher...if you're willing to learn.

14
Take the field to win

 I WANT TO SHARE something important with you. It has to do with counting our blessings, and I think it's especially important today, because I get a sense that many of us are taking an awful lot of things for granted. We seem to be in an "I feel sorry for myself" syndrome, and that kind of attitude is destructive. It leads nowhere and often can bring about defeat.

What brings on this phenomenon? The loss of a job, a business not doing so well, or a rough spot in a marriage are some of the things that can happen to bring on self-pity. If anything like that is happening to you, don't succumb to feeling sorry for yourself. Instead, take stock and realize how lucky you are.

Start by taking a look at your health. If you have that, you've got something a lot of other people would give their eyeteeth for.

And how about friends? If you have only one friend, you've got something very precious.

How about family? The love and support of family members means everything, but too often we don't see it.

And how about your job? If you have one, what a great privilege to be able to work. But too often when I see people in action on their jobs, they complain so much about what they do that they kind of miss the whole point of what working and living are all about.

How about freedom? You can say and do just about anything. You don't need a pass to travel to another state. And if you just want to goof off, there's no one to stop you.

We all have an abundance of options, but everything I've just mentioned is taken for granted by individuals who should know better.

I often hear things like, "I'm only one person. What can I do?" I then tell the story of Karl Bays, the great salesman who formerly headed American Hospital Supply Co. When the company was bought out by Baxter, he became chairman of that conglomerate before heading up Whitman Industries. Mr. Bays had an inscription on his wall that went something like this: "Spectators will please remove themselves from the playing field." In other words, we're all part of a team, and if you don't want to compete, then for goodness sake get out of the game and stay out of the way. The world is filled with spectators, and there's really nothing wrong with that approach if that's the kind of cozy life one chooses to live. It does take a lot of the wear and tear out of living, but it also takes out much of the joy and excitement.

The playing field is for men and women who want to make a difference, who want to bring about change, who want to be heroes. They want to make things happen. They don't wallow in self-pity, and they don't take things for granted.

Not taking things for granted is part of being a doer and a winner. It has to do with commitment, enthusiasm, and passion— all essential ingredients in the formula for success.

I know learned people who will tell you how bad things are even when they're in the middle of a boom. They just can't bear to see things going well and people feeling good about what they're doing. They're the cynics who think they're so much smarter than the rest of us. Tell all of the naysayers to go jump in a lake, and then you go jump on the field of action.

The playing field is where you'll find the fun and excitement. Sure, you'll get bruised and even bloodied at times, but life is meant to be fought by heroes—people who want to excel. Sitting on the sidelines feeling sorry for yourself isn't the way to do it. A positive attitude is everything. Get into the middle of things and make a difference. It's the surest way to success. Come on, realize your dreams!

15
The case of the Tin Man, or, Why it's important to have a heart

THE HUMAN HEART is amazing. Think of what it does on a daily basis to keep us alive. They say that sometime in the future, there will be an artificial heart that will work just like the real thing. I guess we'll just have to wait and see on that one.

I'm writing about the heart because of thoughts brought to mind by a presentation I heard at a CEO retreat. One CEO was discussing why a proposed merger involving her hospital fell apart. As she was talking about what went wrong, she put a drawing of the human heart on the screen, and that caught my attention. With that picture, she was trying to convey that the proposed merger didn't work out mainly because the two CEOs involved in the deal differed dramatically in terms of how they ran their hospitals. Even though they had agreed that a merger of their facilities was a good thing, when they tried to put the deal together, irreconcilable conflicts arose between the two CEOs and their colleagues. They had lost heart.

That picture of the heart keeps coming back to me. Remember the Tin Man in *The Wizard of Oz*? He longed for a heart so that he could feel things such as love, sadness, and happiness. There are so many attributes of the heart.

In many cases, the heart is used figuratively to describe these concepts. We often say someone "has a good heart" when that person shows empathy or seems to care deeply about the human condition. Or we'll say a person "has heart" when he or she has shown great courage. Or how about the concept of love, as when a person is said to have a "broken heart."

The heart means many things to many people, and it's used all the time to convey feelings. That's the one thing no test can measure. Sure, there are tests that tell you whether your heart is healthy or not, or whether it's physically large or small, but I'm talking about the things that defy measurement, the things going on inside someone beyond the physiological.

Unfortunately, I think too many of us have become immune to the condition of other people's hearts, because many of us spend so much time breaking them. We forget that everyone has feelings. Think what life would be like without someone to love. Think what life would be like if you didn't have the heart to pursue excellence. Think how empty life would be if you didn't commit your heart to projects dear to you. It's called giving your all. It's one person making a difference.

I know a lot of people who have a heart, but they don't use it. They don't commit themselves to anything. If it's to be used properly, the heart has to be used constantly to feel joy and sorrow, triumph and failure. But too many of us miss out. Get committed! Get on with it! Use your heart to its fullest every day.

Many successful people have well-developed hearts, because they know what a strong heart can accomplish. They've used their hearts to sell products. They've used their hearts to make others happy.

Oh, by the way, if your heart is broken, it has the uncanny ability to heal itself—over time.

Finally, take heart when people tell you that you can't accomplish something. They simply have no idea what kind of heart you have, so they don't know how determined you can be.

How you treat others

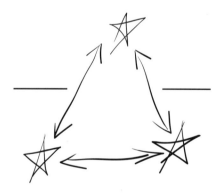

16

Better than "Open, sesame": Some other magic words that will open doors

THERE ARE MAGICAL WORDS that can make all the difference in the world, but too many of us hesitate to use them. They can open doors. They can start meaningful relationships. They can make someone's day. And those are just some of the things a few well-chosen words can bring about. But something seems to have happened to us as we go about the business of day-to-day living. We have forgotten how to be civil with one another. Apparently we're in such a hurry that we forget how important it is to take time to be decent human beings. Oh, I know, these are the '90s, and this is a fast-paced world. But are we really all that busy?

I'm referring to words such as *thank you, please, may I?,* and *I'm sorry* that shouldn't be in such short supply in a civilized society.

When I'm not traveling, I always have a cup of coffee and an English muffin at what could be termed a greasy spoon in my hometown before I head downtown to the office. It helps me gear up for the rigors of the day. But what gets to me is how rude so many people are to the waitress. Seldom do I hear a customer say please while placing an order. Politeness is simply a nice touch and shows respect for someone who's willing to serve us. And it's good manners.

But maybe we're getting away from that type of thinking. Maybe we want to be curt with each other. Maybe I'm just overreacting. No, I don't think so. I believe everyone deserves to be treated with dignity and respect. A simple please or thank you

39

should be second nature. Should we really need to be reminded to be polite?

Consider the words *thank you*. Why is it that so many of us have such a tough time getting those words out? It doesn't take much effort. Yet managers forget to thank their employees. Those of us in business forget to thank our customers. Husbands and wives forget to say thank you to each other. Friends forget to say to each other, "Thank you for being you." It's not a painful thing to do, and just think how you'd stand out in this rude society we live in.

Are we too inhibited, or have we just forgotten to be pleasant with each other? Are we so busy and so important that we just don't want to honor others with simple courtesies? Words such as *please* and *excuse me* are about basic decency. And that's what being a good person is all about. That's also what good citizenship is about.

Try a few of those words on others just as an experiment. Try saying please when you need help from a stranger. Try "I'll have the ham and eggs, please," next time you order. Try saying please when you want something from one of your colleagues or a family member. But make sure you mean it! Few people can resist someone who adds a sincere please.

Think about your own experiences when others treat you with dignity and respect. It stands out simply because someone has taken the time to be considerate of you. Successful salespeople know all about the power of good manners. If they hadn't employed good manners, they wouldn't have reached first base in their careers. In many cases it separates the winners from the losers.

So, if you're not doing so already, start using some of those words that can make a person's day. *Please* say them often, and let them do their magic.

17

Brevity shows respect for others

WE ALL HAVE TIME PRESSURES. There just never seem to be enough hours in a day. That's because we're all so busy. Busy doing our jobs. Busy taking care of our families. Busy trying to be better citizens. Those of us who travel a great deal have even more demands on our time. We're continually dashing to and from airports and rushing to make appointments. When we have time, we guard it jealously, because it means we can try to get certain things done that we've put off too many times. It's a vicious circle. But this brings me to the point of this little essay. It has to do with time manners. Let me explain.

Brevity stands out. But a lot of people don't seem to have a clue. If they get you on the phone, you just know you're doomed for a good forty-five minutes or more. So you try to avoid their calls. Then there are the salespeople who come in, make presentations, and act as though they have the whole day to sell you something. Or the after-dinner speakers who don't know when to sit down. How many times have you heard someone say, "That speech was too short"? If you have, then I would say you're one in a million. On the other hand, how many times have you heard complaints about a speech or presentation lasting far too long?

There's simply too much hot air around. Some individuals seem to love to hear themselves talk. Many speakers think that what they have to say is so special that no one could possibly object if they go over their allotted time by a good half-hour or so. That kind of insensitivity borders on rudeness.

Whatever the situation, my advice is to err on the side of brevity when dealing with others. Don't bore people with endless conversations and discussions about everything but the subject at hand. When writing, keep the memo or letter tight. When giving a

41

talk, don't ramble on. Let people know at the beginning where you're going, and then get there as quickly as you can. If you're going to make a presentation to a customer, ask up front how much time you have, and abide by that limit. You'll be admired for your discipline and consideration, and you'll probably be invited back.

Great communicators seem to have a sixth sense about how much time they can take in any given situation. In short, they know when to quit. They make sure they don't overstay their welcome. In everything we do, we should be conscious of the time element.

Meetings, for instance, should always be brief and to the point, but, more often than not, they last too long and waste everyone's time. I urge you to avoid becoming a "meetings person." If you must have a meeting, keep everyone standing, say what you need to say, and then let everyone get back to work.

Good manners are so rare today that when you observe them, you can't help but be impressed. That's especially true when it comes to respecting each other's time. Remember, it's a precious commodity for all of us.

18
The essence of good manners

MANNERS MIRROR THE CHARACTER of an individual. Good manners make us civilized and are the essence of decency. But in today's hectic world, too many of us have forgotten how important it is to employ good manners in our day-to-day encounters with others. We're just too busy being busy to think of others. We don't take the time to open a door or to listen to the thoughts and opinions of those around us. To me, these things are signs of depth. When you see people with good manners, they stand out like beacons in the night.

So it was with a great deal of interest that I read a *Wall Street*

Journal article on the topic of manners. It was an interview with Letitia Baldrige, who's considered one of the country's top experts on manners. Ms. Baldrige has written books on the subject, including *Letitia Baldrige's Complete Guide to the New Manners for the '90s* (Rawson, 1990), and she writes a syndicated advice column, "R.S.V.P." She has also written *Letitia Baldrige's New Complete Guide to Executive Manners* (Rawson, 1993).

Now, you wouldn't think executives should need too many reminders on manners, but believe me, that's not so. A few years ago, I had lunch with the CEO of a large corporation, and of course when someone has reached that level, you at least expect him to have fundamental manners such as knowing how to use a knife and fork. Not in this case. When lunch arrived and we began to eat, this high-powered executive started shoveling his food onto his fork with his hand. It was somewhat distracting, to say the least, and just goes to show why we need more teachers like Ms. Baldrige.

In the *Wall Street Journal* article, Ms. Baldrige gives her observations about the state of good manners today. "It's consideration and kindness and thinking about somebody other than oneself," she said. "Mind you, there's a difference between a greasy, obsequious, slathering fool who thinks he has good manners and…somebody who is naturally, easily good-mannered, like George Washington."

Where did Ms. Baldrige get started on the good manners trail? It began when she was a little girl and her mother and father taught her what good manners were all about. Her dad, a Republican congressman from Nebraska, was a stickler for good manners, especially at the dinner table. Whenever she and her two brothers acted up at the table, there was a strict ten-minute period of silence imposed by their father. Mother, on the other hand, taught the children how important it was to write thank-you notes and condolence letters. When the children had completed their notes, she would escort them to the corner mailbox, and as the letters went in, she would simply say, "Now, doesn't that feel good?"

At the tender age of twenty-one, Ms. Baldrige became social secretary at the U.S. Embassy in Paris, where she learned the intricacies of protocol. After a two-year stint in the CIA in the early

43

1950s, she became Jackie Kennedy's chief of staff and social secretary to the White House. She has paid her dues, and she knows how important good manners are no matter what the situation.

But her definition of good manners—so simple and so basic—keeps coming back to me. It's being courteous to everyone you meet. It's writing a note to give a word of encouragement or to tell someone how much sorrow you feel at the loss of a loved one. It's waiting until everyone at your table is seated—especially the ladies—before seating yourself. All kinds of things. All kinds of courtesies. Maybe you think they're no big deal, but they show respect for others, and they set you apart.

Believe me, when people see good manners, they not only admire the person who shows them, but they're also likely to emulate them. Good manners lead to more good manners and make us better people.

As grandmother used to say, good manners will open all kinds of doors. Go ahead, turn the handle.

19
Humor and humility make a winning tandem

I DON'T KNOW ABOUT YOU, but I enjoy being around people who try to have fun no matter what they're doing. And there's nothing I admire more than a good sense of humor. I've said it many times before—I believe that humor is crucial to success, whether in business or any other facet of life.

Yet there are still those who simply don't get it or, worse still, those who don't want to get it. They're the sticks-in-the-mud. Levity in any given situation befuddles them. I also believe a well-developed sense of humor mirrors a person's intelligence. I can't prove that scientifically, but from my personal experience, most of the people I know who have a good sense of humor are a cut above those who don't.

According to an article in *Communication Briefings*, humor can help one succeed in the workplace. Some interesting statistics were cited in the article. For instance, in a study of one hundred executives at some of the country's largest corporations, 84 percent thought employees with a sense of humor do a better job than those with little sense of humor. But the eye-opener came when a survey of 737 chief executives of large corporations found that 98 percent said they look for a good sense of humor when they're hiring.

Humor is a tricky thing. It often has a lot to do with the time and place. I've known people who could tell a joke and have everyone in the room waiting for the punch line. Yet there are others who can tell the same joke, and nobody even bothers to wait for the end of the story. I think some of us just need more practice than others.

We also have to be careful how we use it. Using humor to belittle others is never appropriate. And telling off-color stories doesn't belong either. It only spells disaster.

Humor, used appropriately, definitely can be a very valuable tool in business. Some of the most successful salespeople I know always have a bevy of jokes ready in order to break the ice when they go on calls. People like funny stories and folks who can make them laugh. There's no big surprise there.

Remember that humor is more than just a laugh. It has a lot to do with how one is perceived and how well one communicates. Most great public speakers I know start their presentations with an amusing story, almost always capturing their audience at the start. It may take practice, but it's worth the effort. And even if you bomb, you can rely on your good humor to bail you out.

That brings me to my final point. The best humor of all is the ability to laugh at oneself. Individuals who can do that show

45

humility, openness, and self-confidence. And people are attracted to others who exhibit those characteristics. Look around, and you'll see the evidence. Humor and success go together.

So don't be afraid to display your sense of humor. It might just be the smartest business decision you'll ever make.

20
Winners don't knock the competition

I LIKE COMPETITION! It keeps me motivated and hustling. It's what the game of life is all about.

There are those who like to compete and others who like to sit on the sidelines as spectators. But if you want to make your mark in the world, you need to be a competitor. The rewards go to those who get out on the field of battle every day and give a full measure of enthusiasm and drive. Those are the ones who make things happen, and without their creativity and dedication, companies don't prosper.

One disturbing trend I have noticed in recent years is the tendency of some salespeople to take an aggressively negative attitude toward their competitors. They tell their clients and prospects what's wrong with the products and services their competitors sell and become so preoccupied with their attack that they forget to tell the good points about their own products.

My position is different: Every professional salesperson's code of conduct should be imprinted with the words, *Never knock your competition*. Slamming them may bring short-term sales, but in the long run it will hurt you badly. Every time you knock your competition, you are not only mentioning their name, but you also are insulting the person you are calling on. You are saying, consciously or unconsciously, that your customer doesn't have the intelligence to make his or her own decisions about your competitors. Knocking

46

the competition is a sign that you are unprofessional and that you lack ethics.

I once made a presentation about *Modern Healthcare* to a group of divisional heads on the East Coast. During my presentation, I didn't mention our competition. Instead, I talked about all the positive things I could think of about our editorial product, our circulation, and our readership. In other words, I put our best foot forward with as much enthusiasm as I could muster.

Later, when I returned to Chicago, I received an urgent call from the head marketing person at the company. "You got our business," he told me. "And we are going to run with you exclusively. Your competitor came in earlier in the week and did nothing but talk about your book in a negative fashion. It was a disaster. Nobody said anything, but we all felt the same way. By knocking you so much, they made you the star of the show. We lost respect for them."

Please think of that. Be positive and win; be negative and lose. Negative selling is a turnoff, yet many salespeople resort to that kind of tactic, either out of frustration or anger. Never stoop to that level. You only hurt yourself and your integrity.

On the other hand, you shouldn't refuse a request by a client to make a comparison between yourself and a competitor. That would be an insult when the client has specifically sought information. What I deplore is the salesperson who goes on an initial call and tries to build a case around what's wrong with the competition's products. Professionals hate this type of conduct and may even ask you to leave if you engage in it.

Customers like to be around people who are positive and confident. They definitely don't like to be around people who are negative and not sure of themselves. Negative selling shows insecurity and bad training.

So stay away from negative selling, even when it hurts to do so. On the other hand, know your product cold so that when you start talking about what you have to offer, you display confidence, stability, enthusiasm, and ethics. If you do, nine out of ten times you are going to win, and in anybody's league those aren't bad numbers—especially when they translate into commission checks.

21

Lauer at length: Lessons in life for all (as written for my grandchildren)

THREE BEAUTIFUL BOYS in a little over two years. First it was Charlie Scott, then Theodore Joseph, and then Matthew Thomas. It's hard to put into words the thrill and joy of it all. I'm the proudest grandpa in the world.

Charlie Scott Lauer, we welcomed you to the United States of America on April 21, 1993—all 4 pounds and 12 ounces of you!

Theodore Joseph has a nice rhythm to it. Theodore Joseph Lauer, my second grandson, was born May 2, 1994, all 6 pounds and 4 ounces of a miracle.

Matthew Thomas Lauer, weighing 7 pounds 9 ounces and stretching 21 inches, was born May 19, 1995. What a beautiful miracle—and what a wonderful birthday present for me!

I was just outside the delivery room when each of you were born. I heard your first cries. Every time I see you, I want to hug and kiss you, but you'll get plenty of that from your mom and dad. Of course, I'll have my turn, too.

If I may, I'd like to share some thoughts with you from my perspective as a grandfather—things I've learned over the years that I feel will be important to you sometime in the future as you grow older.

Charlie, Teddy, and Matthew, welcome to the good ole U.S.A. You're going to have some great times. You have been born into a nation that is free, a nation that believes in liberty for all and has the strength and resolve to defend the covenant it has with its citizens. You are among the blessed in this crazy world of ours, born free citizens of a nation that's a beacon of hope for the rest of the world. Don't ever take that freedom for granted, and don't ever take anything else for granted, including the love of all those around you.

The United States is still a young nation, and it has made some mistakes, just as you will as you grow older. But even with all of its faults, this is still the place to be, the greatest country in the world. You can grow up to be anything you want to be. But you have to earn it.

This is a country where you're free to dream your dreams and make them come true. This is a place where opportunity is everywhere. Sometimes we get so caught up in trivia that we overlook the obvious and walk right by it. Keep your eyes and ears open, and you'll do just fine.

Charlie, Teddy, and Matthew, I want you to know that your mom and dad are great people. You are all born out of deep love. Throughout your mother's pregnancies I have never seen two individuals more devoted to each other than your mom and dad. They are very much in love, so when you came along there was nothing but happiness in the delivery room.

You know, boys, real love isn't hard to identify. You can see it in people's faces, and you can see it in the way they touch and kiss. There's a total commitment to one another, and your mother, Wendi, and father, Randy, manifest all the attributes of true love.

One thing I especially want you to know is the way your dad treated your mom just before you decided to join us. I wish you could have seen the compassion, gentleness, and caring your father gave to your mother. Your dad was so tender with your mom, and you could feel the anticipation and joy they were feeling about having you. It's something I will always remember,

49

because it was so basic and so beautiful. Love and gentleness are big items with me, boys, because they are the essence of all that's important in life. The older I get, the more I realize that you can never give enough of yourself to the ones you love.

I was so proud of both of your parents—and I still am and always will be. Now you are here and are about to embark on life's great adventure.

Give every minute of your being 100 percent. Don't wait for things to happen to you. Go out and make things happen. That way you'll make every day a special day, and that's what life is—very special. Don't waste a minute of it.

You'll be surprised how many breaks come your way if you do give 100 percent. Not that it's going to be easy. Life itself is filled with all kinds of pitfalls, but if you work hard and persevere, you'll make it. You will be a success at whatever you do.

Another thing: Nobody owes you anything. Your country certainly doesn't owe you anything. Your mom and dad don't owe you anything except to give you a good start. There are people walking around who think the world owes them a living, but that's a lot of baloney.

Get on the playing field and make your own way. In everything you do, give all the hustle you can muster. If you're enthusiastic and positive, people will beat a path to your door. And you will have fun.

The world may not owe you anything, but you owe the world everything, so give something back every chance you get. Make your own way and never look back. If you can't outthink others, then outwork them. It'll pay off. I know, because I've had to do it myself.

Play by the rules, even though the temptation will be there to cheat. A lot of people do. They cheat in the classroom, they cheat in athletics, they cheat in business. They even cheat their families. But the ultimate irony is that they're cheating themselves most of all.

Don't cheat others, and, just as important, don't cheat yourselves. Because you can't get away from yourselves, Charlie, Teddy, and Matthew. If you cheat at something, you'll have to live with it, and that won't be a good feeling. What satisfaction is there in accomplishing something and knowing in the back of your mind you didn't do it on the square? It will leave you feeling empty and second-rate.

Remember that most people are honest and care about others. Americans are a generous bunch. They love the underdog, and when they see others in trouble, they go out of their way to help. As a matter of fact, the American people give billions of dollars to various charities every year. We've also given billions upon billions to other nations around the world to help the starving and the oppressed. But you'll discover all of this yourselves as you get older.

If you ever get into a position of power, be considerate of others. Don't be a boss; be a colleague and friend to those who look to you for leadership. Be gentle and caring. That's important in everything you do. Always give people hope and look on the bright side, because life is so precious and there is so little time.

You'll have some tough times as the years go by. Everybody has them. But they help a person grow. If life were easy and there were no challenges, we wouldn't develop character. And character is so important. It's what makes us special. Character involves treating your mom and dad with respect. It involves keeping your word and playing by the rules. It involves caring about others. It involves being loyal to God, country, and yourself.

Don't be afraid to believe in God and the power of prayer. I pray for you, your mom and dad, and everybody I can think of every night. It has helped me through some tough times. It'll do wonders for you too.

Learn early on to respect yourselves. If you don't, you'll never really enjoy life. And the only way I know to gain self-respect is always to strive to be good citizens. People who care for themselves care for those around them as well.

Always remember the love of your mother and father. You only have one of each, and they are special, so treat them well. Be assured that you will always be in their hearts.

Finally, boys, a friend of mine once told me there are only three things in life that really count: love of family, love of friends, and love of work. That's what it's all about. Remember that if you want somebody to be your friend, you have to go out of your way to be a friend. In other words, reach out to others and they will reach out to you.

Profiles in personal success

22
Profile of Carrie Ponder: Ph.D. in what matters most

 A STORY I READ in 1991 marked the second time I had heard about an exceptional woman and her family. The first time was in an issue of the *Chicago Tribune*, and the second time it was a story in *USA Today*. Anybody who reads about Carrie Ponder as I did can't help but come away both stimulated and inspired. She triumphed over virtually impossible odds and reared eight children in Chicago's inner city. Her children have been educated in such preeminent universities as Princeton, Northwestern, the University of Chicago, and five other fine schools.

Carrie Ponder is one of those individuals not easily intimidated. Think of a single mother earning about $10,000 a year even dreaming of raising and educating eight children, let alone putting them all through college. Montie Blackman, a former development director at the Midwest Women's Center, said about Carrie Ponder: "She...never gave up. Her success in keeping her children together and instilling the value of education in them makes her a perfect role model."

How did she manage to do all this? By doing domestic work and using her sewing skills. Other jobs included counseling battered women. Ms. Ponder also gives credit to her church, the library, and programs in her community. But according to the *USA Today* article, she networked all the time. "You're constantly talking to people. People asked how I raised eight children alone," she said. "No, I did not raise eight children alone. There's the church, your neighbors, your friends, the library, all kinds of organizations. People I don't even know were part of the process."

She took advantage of every opportunity she could find, and taught her kids to do the same.

Her son Reginald, the Princeton graduate who went on to become an advertising executive, had this to say about his mother's attitude: "We were taught early on that if we want something, we have to go out and get it. We have to be vocal, we have to be aggressive, we have to push. We'd see that in her, because if we wanted another pair of shoes, she would go out and get another job. The lesson was: You could get what you want, you just have to work for it, and you have to work hard."

And then Carrie Ponder added this: "If you can't get what you want on this corner, there's always another corner to turn. It's like when you go for a job, you knock on many doors, and they say no. But you just keep knocking if that's what you want."

There are many Carrie Ponders in these United States. They should inspire every last one of us. They simply go out and take advantage of every opportunity. Carrie Ponder's story is proof that hard work and knocking on doors do pay off.

Reading about Carrie Ponder was inspirational. I'm inspired by her perseverance, character, and determination. Think of what she's given to her children and to this nation—eight bright, productive citizens who are making creative and worthwhile contributions to society by following the example of their mother.

The *USA Today* article says Carrie Ponder is a high school graduate with one year of college. But to my way of thinking, her real-life experiences and accomplishments entitle her to Ph.D.'s in philosophy, education, business, and family life. May her dreams for herself and her family all come true.

23

Profile of Edwin Rose: What you can learn from a pet-food taster

THERE ARE PLENTY OF PEOPLE who are totally dedicated to their jobs. I'm talking about individuals who go the extra mile and then some. They give 100 percent every day simply because they love what they're doing. But it was with some surprise and even a little amazement that I read in the *Wall Street Journal* about one man's dedication. His name is Edwin Rose, and he was identified in the article as a pet-food taster with Britain's Safeway Stores. His story is a classic.

Mr. Rose has been around the food business for some time. Not long ago, he used to select olive oils for Safeway, but he soon lost enthusiasm for that job. "The olive-oil taste would just stick in your mouth," he told the *Journal*. At another time and with a competing supermarket chain, Mr. Rose was a fish buyer. But then Mr. Rose found a niche more to his taste. This all happened when Safeway asked Mr. Rose to establish a line of dog and cat foods. Well, he has gone about doing so by making sure he tastes each and every pet food under development. He gives his competitors' products a taste test as well.

Mr. Rose has become an enthusiast for the chain's pet foods. Simply put, he believes in his products and tells anyone who will listen just how delicious and appetizing pet food can be. That's because the products are made under stringent controls. As Mr. Rose puts it, they're "pasteurized, sterilized and every other 'ized."

So what does he recommend? "I must confess," he said, "the premium cat foods are my favorite."

The consumers of Safeway's pet foods seem to concur with Mr. Rose's taste buds, because the pet-food line ranks in the top twenty of the chain's best-selling grocery products. And there's no doubt he takes those consumers very seriously. He's conscientious almost to a fault. He actually worries that the food he eats at home may interfere with his pet-food palate. "I must pay attention to how much garlic my wife puts in my dinner the night before," he points out.

As far as Mr. Rose's eating habits are concerned, his wife says he isn't a picky eater, fancying a variety of dishes. He especially enjoys chicken. "So does our cat," she adds, "so I've often got the two of them in the kitchen, going at the same bowl."

Because of his dedication, Mr. Rose has gained notoriety in the United Kingdom's pet-food industry. Two sales representatives from a dry pet-food company came to see him about the possibility of stocking their line on Safeway's shelves. They were also interested in seeing if the stories they had heard about Mr. Rose were true. He didn't disappoint them. In the middle of their conversation, he dipped his hand into a bowl of their flaky dog food and started chewing it. One of the sales reps said: "In twenty-five years in the pet-food business, I can honestly say I never saw a buyer eat the product. It shows an overwhelming interest in his area, a curiosity beyond the norm."

So there you have it. Edwin Rose, pet-food taster. Many years ago, when I was trying to figure out what I wanted to be, my father told me: "Whatever you do, try to be the best. If you want to be a ditch digger, then be the best there is. If you want to be a firefighter, be the best there is. Whatever it is you decide to do, give every day 100 percent." Mr. Rose does just that.

I think his unique vocation also demonstrates how many opportunities there are for all of us if we will only learn to recognize them. Go ahead, look around you!

24

Profile: The gentleman in 3-A and the meaning of success

 SUCCESS FOR SOME PEOPLE is accruing money and material things. For others, it's simply showing up at the job every day and doing an honest day's work. Or maybe it's hitting a home run, shooting a three-pointer from the perimeter, or scoring the winning goal on a breakaway in overtime. There are different definitions of success, and all have some validity. The oddity of life is that some individuals who have accomplished so much don't understand how successful they are in the eyes and hearts of others.

This came home to me during a flight from Chicago to Salt Lake City. I was off to speak to a group on the topic of leadership, and I was looking forward to talking about how many opportunities abound for risk takers and entrepreneurs. But on the plane I encountered someone who, in my opinion, is one of the most successful people I have ever met.

Let's call this person the gentleman in 3-A. I had the aisle seat and was busily working on my talk as the fellow took his seat next to me. I was a little preoccupied trying to make a few notes for my speech, so I didn't really notice the man until we were well into the flight. But eventually I got my notes organized and then leaned back to relax a little. And you know how things go. I asked the man next to me if his home was in Salt Lake City. No, he told me, his home was in Wyoming. We began to chat about a variety of topics, such as our families and our jobs. The man, who worked as director of facilities planning on an Indian reservation, told me he had been in Chicago to visit his oldest son.

As we talked, he wanted to know what I did, and I told him I

58

was the publisher of a weekly business magazine covering the health care industry. After a little more talk, I took a nap.

When I awoke, we picked up where we had left off, and that's when he told me about his son in Chicago. Apparently his son had become cynical about life and during their conversations he doubted he had been able to turn his son's thinking around. This gentleman was really feeling down and asked me what I thought. That's when I asked him about the rest of his family. He told me he and his wife had raised three sons and that he was very proud of them. He had been married to his wife for about thirty-six years, and I could tell he was proud of her as well.

And then he talked about being a foster parent. He and his wife had taken in the first boy when he was only five months old, and they had been warned that the child might not live very long because he had been brutally abused. As the gentleman in 3-A told the story, he related how this Indian baby had fooled everyone and lived to five-and-a-half years. There were tears in his eyes—and in mine.

Then he told me about their latest foster son. The boy, who had fetal alcohol syndrome, had joined them a few years earlier at the age of seven. He and his wife hoped to adopt the boy soon. As is common with children who have fetal alcohol syndrome, there had been some traumatic episodes of uncontrollable screaming and even violence, but things seemed to be straightening out.

I wish you could have been there with me to hear this man's story. Aside from the tears over the death of the five-year-old, the fellow related his story in a rather matter-of-fact way. In short, he didn't seem to understand the impact he was having on me. It was as though it was a pretty routine matter for a couple to raise three boys on an Indian reservation, send them off into the world, and then turn right around and take in two foster children with multiple problems instead of sitting back, kicking off their shoes, and relaxing.

Thank goodness there are people like this in our midst. How much richer we are because of them.

And there's probably no better definition for success. This wonderful man and his wife are what it's really all about—giving to your fellow human beings and making this world a better place.

Principles
of
success in action

"Success, like anything else, has to be planned for. It can't be a last-minute thing....It has to be taken as seriously as any other long-term strategy."

uccess is not a static concept sealed in a vacuum. It's a dynamic, active reality that permeates the pursuits of everyday life. Success is far more than just not failing, just as vibrant health is far more than not being sick. Success is not only rising above the negative but achieving the positive.

In this section, you'll have an opportunity to see success at work in the arenas of management and leadership, sales and marketing, and customer service.

To realize success, we must not only study it but practice it. We must not only think about it but act on it.

A wish—a desire—to succeed is commendable. But unless we translate desire into action—unless we abandon the sideline benches for the playing field—we cannot fulfill our dreams.

Making your organization shine:

SUCCESS IN

MANAGEMENT

AND LEADERSHIP

. . . .

*"Leaders must care deeply about others
and make the commitment to take care of
fellow workers and subordinates.
Leaders must be consummate cheerleaders....
Leaders love to see others win and succeed."*

Leadership isn't about power and authority. It's about knowing how to motivate people to give their best to an organization.

It's about clarifying goals and missions, then communicating them to a workforce so clearly and consistently that everyone feels inspired to reach them. It's about increasing productivity through a charged-up workforce eager to tackle challenges when the workday begins.

Management doesn't begin with budgets and bottom lines. It begins with people. It seeks to maximize the potential of all employees, to channel their energies and creativity into achieving amazing results.

Qualities of stellar managers and leaders

25
Traits of a good leader in the '90s

 LEADERSHIP IN THE 1990s seems to be taking on a whole new perspective, and it's a good thing. At the same time, many who once thought that being a leader was the thing to do are opting out of that pursuit, for they realize they don't want to endure the stress it brings. But that brings us to an even more important point: What constitutes a good leader?

Is the individual tall or short, brilliant or average, good-looking or plain? Does the person have a graduate degree or any degree? Just what are the things that count if one is going to lead effectively—especially during these challenging times? I think you'll find that leaders come in all shapes and sizes. For what really matters, you need to look at what's inside.

Let's start with some basics. Humility has to be one of the most crucial traits of any leader. Those who want to lead need the ability to look at themselves objectively and not take themselves too seriously. There's too much ego and false pride in the workplace these days. People forget from whence they came and, consequently, forget those who helped them get where they are. If people who report to you don't trust you and think of you as a phony, they'll find it hard to level with you. More important, they'll probably refuse to follow you.

Then there's something else that means so much if you truly want to be a leader. I'm talking about treating others with dignity and respect. Great leaders do this all the time. People are nuts about bosses who not only have humility but go out of their way to be thoughtful and caring. To fire someone is easy, but to take someone who has lost his or her way and enthusiasm, then turn them around and get them on the ball again demonstrates real leadership ability. It's also good business. But it takes patience and courage to behave this way. Firing someone is the easy way out. The manager who can rekindle that fire in a person is to be admired.

Then we get into the issue of empowerment. It's letting people do their thing, giving them your trust and confidence, and acting as a cheerleader when they stumble. That's leadership. No one comes to work in the morning wanting to do a bad job. Most people want to do their very best, but all too often when they hit the front door, the environment is so negative and the atmosphere so clogged with internal politics that they get turned off and simply give up. That's when the leader who cares comes in.

Don't tolerate petty politics, and don't play favorites. Leaders must be above the crowd. They have to set standards, which means they have to be above board in all dealings with their colleagues. Character, ethics, and morality are all part of effective leadership, but are too often forgotten. Character means being a square shooter and setting an example for the rest of the organization. Tolerating any kind of cheating, or looking the other way when something is handled improperly, isn't the way to set values for the people who report to you. To my way of thinking, character, ethics, and morality are intertwined. There's no easy way out.

Yes, being a leader is tough. Leaders must be mentors, not competitors. Leaders must care deeply about others and make the commitment to take care of fellow workers and subordinates. Leaders must be consummate cheerleaders but also be willing to endure criticism, loneliness, and isolation. It may sound glum, but it doesn't have to be, because true leaders take great joy in the success of others. That's the secret. Leaders love to see others win and succeed. If you don't feel that way, don't get into the business of leading, because you're probably too wrapped up in yourself to understand what sacrifices leadership requires.

Touching someone's life by showing them the road to success is special, and real leaders understand that. Come to think of it, that's what life is all about—caring for others and helping them along the way.

So, if you want to be a leader, start now by learning all you can about working and dealing with others. Part of that is being a good listener and making others feel they're the most important people in your life when you're with them. It's all part of the package. Helping others become stars in their own right—that's part of reaching out and becoming a star yourself.

26
Don't get in the way of your stars

AS ANY OF YOU who read my column know, I believe in the empowerment of people in the workplace—in other words, giving individuals the freedom to do their jobs. Some enlightened companies follow this philosophy, but others are headed by so-called leaders who still believe the way to get people to do something is to rule by fear or fiat. While that approach might find some success in the short term, in the long run it only stifles the ideas, creativity, and ingenuity that can emerge if people are given unfettered opportunities to do their jobs. That's not to mention the turnover you're likely to see. Over time, organizations only succeed by keeping their most productive workers.

So it was with some pleasure that I read an anecdote recounted in the *Speaker's Idea File*, published by Ragan Communications. The story, culled from Bruce Nash and Allan Zullo's Sports Hall of Shame, goes like this: During a tense 1985 NBA game, Boston Celtics coach K.C. Jones called time-out and diagrammed a play in the huddle—only to have superstar Larry Bird say, "Get the ball to me and get everyone out of my way." Mr. Jones responded, "I'm the coach, and I'll call the plays!" Then he turned to the other players and said, "Get the ball to Larry and get out of his way."

That little story says a lot. Coach Jones had to be one heck of a leader. He had brains enough to listen to one of his star performers and follow his lead. He also displayed a great sense of humor and a well-developed sense of humility. He could have been a jerk about the whole incident but instead chose to give his players the benefit of the doubt and just let them do their jobs.

The story demonstrates everything I try to tell people about leadership. It's not about false pride. It's not about being competitive with one's colleagues. And it's not about giving others orders they don't necessarily want to follow. Leadership is about letting people know they have the latitude to perform the way they see fit. Leadership is treating others with dignity and respect. Leadership involves humor, humility, and hard work.

That, to me, pretty well describes true leadership for the '90s and beyond. But too many companies just don't get it. Too many of them still look at their employees from an adversarial point of view—they are to be distrusted, feared, and corralled. That attitude spells failure. No organization, no company, no team can succeed without good people. But good people need nurturing and a sense of mission from their leaders. They need leaders who care and who exude commitment.

Ethics are involved, too—ethics in the treatment of each other and in the treatment of customers. I'd like to think most of us still believe in the basic principles we were raised with—playing by the rules and giving every day our best.

Think of a place where excellence is encouraged and where you can be yourself and have the freedom to get the job done, where you're respected and treated with courtesy by enlightened management. How many of us work in this type of environment? If you do, you're associated with a true winner. But don't take it for granted. There are thousands, maybe millions, working for companies that simply don't give a darn about freedom, dignity, and respect. That's tragic.

Right now people are crying out for leadership. They're confused and worried about their jobs and the future of their industry. True leaders need to come forward and help with these concerns by offering a mission and a vision.

You can show the way by following the example of K.C. Jones. Listen to your stars, be receptive to their ideas, and then get out of their way so they can get the job done.

27
Humor boosts morale

 HUMOR IN THE WORKPLACE is essential to good morale, but too many managers really don't understand the crucial role it plays. That's such a basic concept, but for some reason its relevance seems to have escaped the intellect of a lot of people—from top executives on down. Without humor and laughter, the world wouldn't be a very enjoyable place. Think about it. What *would* it be like without laughter? What if we seldom heard the giggles of children or that contagious laughter of a friend? It's all part of life—and so essential to our well-being. And that's especially true at our jobs, since work accounts for so much of our time.

As a salesman, I've walked into places where you could cut the tension with a knife. I've seen it all. Surly people. Employees with zero morale. People basically not enjoying one of the great privileges of day-to-day life—working. It shouldn't be that way, but such companies aren't hard to find.

Who do you blame, and why should this be happening, especially when we're all supposed to be more enlightened about these situations? The blame lies at the top. It all starts with the boss's ego, because, as a rule, people with big egos take themselves far too seriously. Individuals with big egos tend to be insensitive to everyone but themselves. For them, life is centered on a single letter—I. "I did this," or "I did that," or "I'm responsible for the success of this project or that product."

We've all heard these people sound off about how important they are and how things would fall apart without them. The words *we* or *us* don't seem to be part of their vocabularies. What they don't understand is that without their colleagues, they wouldn't or couldn't accomplish anything. I call these people the "me me" crowd. How sad that they have power over anyone's life.

70

Yes, humor has everything to do with this. It may not come out of a textbook, and it probably isn't taught in most graduate schools of business, but it's tough to teach street smarts and common sense, both of which are embodied in having the intelligence to approach life with good humor. I'm not talking about slapstick comedy in the workplace or ill-timed and embarrassing practical jokes—just clean fun and a willingness to laugh at yourself and even have the humility to allow others to make you the butt of a joke once in a while. One of the traits of all effective leaders is a well-developed sense of humor, not only about life but about themselves. That's key to effective leadership in the '90s.

Look at other companies. People want to work for those with leaders who are quick with a smile and who show a sense of humor. No one wants to work at a place so filled with tension and pressure that there's no joy to be found. Finding ways to have some fun should be encouraged in every place of employment, because it's one of the simplest ways to improve productivity. Study after study has found that laughter might be the best medicine for any situation. If your company is ailing, maybe a little levity is just what the doctor ordered. But again, it all starts at the top, and until the boss understands this basic concept, he or she runs the risk of failure.

Sounds so simple, doesn't it? Simple humor and simple humility. But in today's world, where so many leaders think of themselves as power brokers, the whole concept I've been talking about is hard to implement if it doesn't already exist in a particular work environment.

If you don't work in a place where you're able to have a good time while doing your job...get out! No matter what they pay you, life is too short. Go to a place where people work with each other and care about each other and where the person at the top leads by example and good humor.

Leaders would do well to remember that if their employees can't have fun doing their jobs, their own success is in jeopardy. Then the joke would be on them.

28

Communication skills essential for effective leadership

 LEADERSHIP IS CRUCIAL to the success of any organization. We've all seen examples of what can happen to a company when leadership is weak. The end result is often failure and the loss of jobs. It's happening all the time, and too frequently the so-called leaders who bring failure to an operation are allowed to leave with big severance packages while the employees are left demoralized and disillusioned.

Of course that's not right, but if a board doesn't take leadership ability seriously enough, often the individual brought in to run the show is someone who appears to possess all the prerequisites of a good manager but lacks that one essential characteristic—knowing how to lead. That may sound pretty basic, but quality leadership is missing all over the place. Just pick up any issue of the *Wall Street Journal* and read about it. Every day there are examples of "leaders" taking a business down the road to disaster—often a very quick trip.

Maybe it's time to take a closer look at leaders today and what makes some effective and others ineffective. Maybe we could all learn something from such an exercise.

Since the subject of leadership has always interested me, I was intrigued by a report I received from a company called Corporate Systems Inc., based in South Bend, Indiana. In preparation for a presentation at the Thirty-seventh Congress of the American College of Healthcare Executives, the firm conducted a study among 540 health care executives. They were sent questionnaires for the informal poll, conducted in February 1994. The leaders were asked three open-ended questions about streamlining management. Some ninety-nine responses were received, representing hospitals of all sizes and from all sections of the country.

What were some of the traits of poor-performing managers? At the top were complacency and comfort with the status quo, cited by 37 percent of the executives. Being controlling and autocratic came in second at 35 percent. Poor communication came next with 30 percent, followed by narrow-mindedness, 27 percent; being inflexible and unwilling to change, 25 percent; protection of turf, 24 percent; tardiness on deadlines/procrastination, 23 percent; being negative or critical, 21 percent; inability to accept responsibility for actions, 20 percent; and indecisiveness, 19 percent. None of these should be surprising, because any of them is one too many for an effective manager.

But what about the characteristics of top leaders? What seems to be the most crucial of all is the ability to communicate. That trait was cited by 46 percent of the respondents, followed by vision/systems orientation at 41 percent. Those two abilities were the ones health care execs found to be the most desirable in today's highly competitive environment. By contrast, coaching/motivating was a distant third with 24 percent. Role modeling was a weak 15 percent, while things such as relationship building and initiative scored only 14 percent.

Those top two traits probably shouldn't surprise us any more than what we learned about the qualities of poor-performing managers. Communication is essential in today's fast-paced business climate. Any leader—in any business—worth his or her salt has to be able to communicate effectively if everyone in the organization is to head in the same direction. But even today many leaders feel that those who report to them will somehow get the picture of what they expect, maybe through osmosis. Well, that just doesn't happen. There's no greater ability than being able to convey—clearly and concisely—your dreams and aspirations for the organization. It's the difference between quality, successful leadership, and lackluster fumbling.

In short, whether in good times or bad, the ability to communicate with colleagues is the one skill in which every effective leader must excel. But that isn't always easy, because it involves being open, honest, and direct. Without communication, morale sags, confusion reigns—and failure isn't far off.

The order of this day and every day should be: communicate, communicate, communicate. None of us does it often enough.

Lauer at length: Five business commandments worth singing about*

I'm singing in the rain,
I'm singing in the rain,
What a glorious feeling,
I'm happy again.

What could possibly have inspired Gene Kelly to sing those words? It's true, it was the 1950s, and things were different then. I should know, because I lived through that era. I returned from the Korean War and started my first job as a salesman.

---

* This piece is excerpted and adapted from a speech originally presented by Charles S. Lauer at a luncheon of chief operating officers in 1995.

It was a time that the *Chicago Tribune* has called the nation's golden era—"prosperous, wholesome, respectful, upwardly mobile, powered by values as simple as black and white." It was the time of *Leave It to Beaver* and *Father Knows Best*, not *Beavis and Butt-Head* and *Ren & Stimpy*.

So the times, in part, explained the optimism that seemed to rush off the screen in movies such as *Singing in the Rain, An American in Paris*, and all the other great musicals.

When you've been around as long as I have, you begin to see the wisdom in the old clichés: Life isn't fair. There's no such thing as a free lunch. Money won't buy happiness. No pain, no gain. Talk is cheap. No man is an island. I know you have heard all these before. Let me give you some of my own. Here are five commonsense pieces of wisdom I've developed on my own about how to sing in the rain no matter what's going on around you.

Commandment I:
Go back to the golden rule and think before you swing the ax

Reengineering, cost cutting, and downsizing are great concepts, at least in theory, but it's easy to throw out the baby with the bath water. It's easy to consolidate and change functions without really thinking about the effects. And it's easy for the people who run organizations to think of employees as "deadwood" or "disposable technology."

That was reflected in a survey released by Challenger, Grey, and Christmas. Nearly 75 percent of the executives polled said that burnout is greater now than twenty years ago. And a majority said that managers are working too many hours, are physically exhausted by the end of the day, and bring too much work home. In other words—whether it's from cost cutting and downsizing, or mergers and acquisitions—people are hurting.

Think about the organizations you've known that went through downsizing and consolidation. How many were open about why and how people got selected for termination or layoffs? How many asked employees for input? How many gave people the option of part-time jobs, or job sharing? And how many made sure that people at the middle and top of the organization were hit with the same force as those at the bottom?

My reading is that just about every organization could do better. Part of the problem is that every one of us has to change the way we look at organizations and at jobs.

Even the architect of reengineering is starting to have second thoughts. In an interview in the *Chicago Tribune*, James Champy says that organizations need to talk less about strategy, structure, and systems and more about people, process, and culture. He tells business people to continually ask questions such as: What business are we in? What's our purpose or mission? What do customers want? Do we have the products to meet those needs?

In other words, before organizations slash, burn, and go for the kill, they need to reflect on the three basic questions of business and life:

Mission: Why are we here?

Vision: Where are we headed?

Values: What do we stand for?

I've probably heard more sad stories in the last year than I have in the last thirty. People in their fifties out of work...with no prospects for a comparable career at a comparable salary. High-level executives having their homes repossessed. Professionals wondering if they'll be able to get their kids through college. The same people who executed layoffs for years now know what it feels like to be on the receiving end of a termination notice.

What I'm saying is that when we make these changes, let's think this through. Ask yourself: How would I want to be treated if I were in the same situation?

Commandment 11: Celebrate success

Sometimes I wonder if people in business really know how to have fun. Cutting budgets and coming up with money-saving ideas is hard work. And that's why I think we have to celebrate every time we knock down a barrier. It might be something as simple as a new form, policy, or procedure, or something as complex as putting in a new information system, or topping off a new building. The important thing is that we celebrate and give as much attention to the little people as we do to the board members and employers.

The choices are endless. Bring people together for coffee and cookies, do-it-yourself ice cream sundaes, or even a special film or video. It doesn't have to be expensive. But be sure to allow plenty of time to give thanks for the past, take your hat off to the present, and look ahead to the future.

In one hospital, senior management decided to put rosebuds on the desks of all of the support staff. It was senior management's way of saying thank-you for the backup and support work done by every employee in that hospital. The roses brightened up the workplace, and employees had a chance to talk about what went on with every person who passed by their desks. And when employees took the bud vases home at the end of the day, they shared their success with their families.

Does that mean we have to buy roses for all of our employees? Of course not. But it does mean we can look for more ways to say thank you. Think about the last carefully selected greeting card or handwritten note you got. Didn't it make you feel good—and didn't you remember the person who wrote it? Most people aren't much different in the way they react to praise.

Commandment III: Take risks

One thing I've learned over the last forty years is that leaders continually stick their necks out—not just to do things right, but also to do the right things. In many cases, they put the mission of the organization before their own welfare. When they stand up to tough-minded board members, they do it with full knowledge that they could be putting their careers on the line. In a tough job market, they know they could soon be out of a job.

One health care executive I know of relocated from a highly competitive market in the Midwest to a slow-to-change market in New England. The entrepreneurial, freewheeling culture he was accustomed to was no more. Change came slowly, and often only after long discussions and painstaking analysis. Still, this executive knew that he had to prepare his organization for integration and managed care and gradually for a move toward consolidation and a merger.

Fortunately, the outcome was positive. The executive was not only successful in executing a merger, but was eventually selected to serve as the president of a major health care system.

But this fellow isn't alone. Everywhere in this country, in every kind of business, executives show the same kind of courage and bravado. In almost every case, they put aside worries about career stability, income, and reputation, to do what's right—for the organization and for the community.

Unfortunately, not all executives fit this mold—and you probably know some of them. Worried about their income, they focus on what makes board members happy. Concerned about their image, they soft-peddle problems and allow them to grow into crises. And even if the organization falls on troubled times, they blame other people or outside forces. In some cases, they bring in a long line of consultants who do little more than hold up the status quo. And when the organization takes a turn for the worse, they quickly jump ship for a greener, more lucrative pasture.

The good news is that those people are in the minority. One of the greatest things you can have going for you is the courage to take on change and make decisions.

Commandment IV: Develop your own definition of success

You've probably heard the remark, "Many people spend their lives climbing the ladder of success only to find that when they get to the top, the ladder is leaning against the wrong building."

Are you one of those people? Did you go into management because you thought it was the path to the top? I've learned that it really doesn't matter if other people think I'm successful. The real question is: Do I think I'm successful? Am I living the life I want to live? Do I have what I need to be happy at least 70 percent of the time?

Look at a book of quotations about success, and you'll find a hundred different opinions. Robert Schuller says, "Success is a journey, not a destination," while Austrian director Josef Von Sternberg once said, "The only way to succeed is to make people hate you."

But it really doesn't matter how Robert Schuller, Donald Trump, or Madonna see success. The real question is: How do I see it? What does it mean to me to live a valuable and worthwhile life?

Should you accept a job that has you traveling most of the time? Well, that depends. Is your idea of success adventure and moving to the top? Or is it being home with your family every night? Should you join a professional organization and devote ten hours a week to it? Well, that depends. Is your idea of success working fourteen hours a day to get a promotion, or getting more involved with your kids or community?

Once you find your own definition of success—as I did for myself—you'll discover that a lot of other decisions will fall into place. I don't think I'll ever forget the editorial I read in the *Wall Street Journal*, written by a rabbi just before Christmas: "Don't sacrifice your family on the altar of career," advised the rabbi. And don't judge yourself "by what you do, but by the meaning that you bring to it." He told the story of simple blue collar people "who transformed their work into a true vocation—a place [where] they could hear the voice of something higher and deeper."

He shared the story of a woman who sold lingerie and whose kindness made a difference in the lives of women who had just had mastectomies, and of a furniture mover who talked lovingly of helping people through the changes in their lives.

"We never know what we do in our work, that will be remembered," wrote the rabbi. "It has nothing to do with our job titles. It has everything to do with [the] faith, vision, and love we bring to it."

Commandment V: Learn to have fun—and learn from your kids

A Chinese philosopher once said, "Choose a job you love, and you'll never have to work another day in your life." For the most part, I think he was right. Every job has its down days, and it's on those days that you have to learn to play at something else.

In a *Wall Street Journal* "Manager's Journal" article he wrote, the fashion designer Karl Lagerfeld talked about the fact that he surrounds himself with music and hundreds of books, magazines, and newspapers every day. In fact, he starts his day reading newspapers—in four different languages. But, most important, he said that he doesn't consider the people who work for him employees, but friends and family. And he wasn't doing a commercial for MCI. "I'm nobody's boss," he wrote, "so I don't have to be bossy."

Would Karl Lagerfeld's approach work as well in other businesses as it does in the world of fashion? Maybe not. But the point is that he's figured out a way to have fun with his work. He knows how to play, even if it's something as simple as picking up an anthology of short stories or putting on a piece of classical music.

We should never lose our sense of play. The *Wall Street Journal* reported the story of a suburban Chicago accounting firm where the top executive frequently wears a gorilla mask and where—during the busiest time of tax season—employees take time off to play miniature golf, shoot darts, or fool around with a Hula Hoop®. The amazing thing is that it seems to be working. Revenues are up, and turnovers are down.

Never forget that the CEO of Ben and Jerry's ice cream got his job not by sending in a résumé or writing the required essay, but by penning a poem, "Time Values and Ice Cream."

Sometimes I think that the most profound lessons in life can come from watching our children. Robert Fulghum put it best when he wrote, "Most of what I really need to know about how to live and what to do and how to be, I learned in kindergarten."

So, when you're wondering about what to do with your division or organization, or how to get along with some of your more difficult colleagues, think about what you tell your kids and grandkids. And remember these words from Fulghum's *All I Really Need to Know I Learned in Kindergarten* (Villard Books, 1989):

"Wisdom was not at the top of graduate school mountain, but there in the sandpile at Sunday School. These are the things I learned: Share everything. Play fair. Don't hit people. Put things where you found them. Clean up your own messes. Don't take things that aren't yours. Say you're sorry when you hurt some-body. Warm cookies and milk are good for you. Live a balanced life. And when you go out into the world, watch for traffic, hold hands, and stick together."

When you're out there in the wild and wonderful business world—and you see the expectations and the problems, the challenges and the temptations, the discouragements and the opportunities—and you start forgetting what you learned in graduate school, just stop and remember kindergarten. The rest will take care of itself.

30
From film stars to sales stars: Use videotape to motivate your sales force

ONE OF THE TOUGHEST things to do with a sales force is to keep the people motivated. Salespeople come in all shapes, sizes, and personalities. Something that will inspire one person won't necessarily have much of an effect on another. So whoever has the responsibility for running a sales team has to be a smart operator. Psychologist, coach, cheerleader, drill sergeant, and friend are just some of the hats a sales leader has to wear in keeping the group highly moti-vated and operating in an efficient manner.

One of the most vital ingredients for a smooth-functioning sales force is sales training. It can mean the difference between being first class and mediocre. Let me explain.

A good friend of mine called to ask if there was something different he could do at his company's annual sales meeting in terms of polishing the skills of various salespeople. While he generally has been very pleased with their performance, he also feels they need a little postgraduate work, so he wanted to know if I had any ideas. My response was for him to try videotaping each of his salespeople giving presentations on their products to another individual. That person could be from outside the company or someone from inside the company who could give an objective analysis.

Sounds simple, doesn't it? Believe me, it isn't. For someone doing a sales pitch, being videotaped can be an intimidating experience. Don't be surprised, if you decide to try it, at the resistance you will run into from some of your sales staff. I'll tell you why.

First of all, each of us has an idea, either consciously or subconsciously, of how others perceive us when we eat, enter a room, or whatever. Some of us may even think we look a little like Robert Redford or Candice Bergen. In other words, we fantasize about how we look and how we behave. The rude awakening comes when you see yourself on videotape. There you are with that hairstyle you thought was so great, but from this angle or that angle it looks like a disaster. Then there's that stylish suit you just bought, but when you see it on the screen, it looks like something you might have picked up at an army/navy store.

But the real rude awakening occurs when you start your sales presentation. Most of us feel pretty sharp when it comes to talking about our products or services to a potential customer. We may even think we're what could be termed *silver tongued*. But again, there you are on videotape, and something seems to have changed. You slur your words, or you forget to bring in certain support materials as you're talking about your product. You may scratch yourself in a strange place, put your hand over your mouth, or enact other bad habits, even though you'd swear you never do those things when you're out on a sales call.

One of the most successful salesmen I ever knew had the habit of hitching his pants up before he sat down to make a sales pitch. I told him about it a number of times, but he continued to do it without realizing it until the day I videotaped him. When he saw the tape, he was appalled. Video shows you as you really are, and sometimes it can be quite shocking. I've even had people break down and cry after seeing themselves on videotape.

Consequently, sales videotaping, even though it's a great teacher, must be used in a judicious manner. It should be an aid, not a weapon. Whoever is doing the grading must remember to have the same criteria for everyone. Those criteria must be worked out before the taping begins, and all salespeople should know what they are. When I use videotaping, I emphasize things like appearance, concision and thoroughness of presentation, listening skills, asking for the order, and good manners.

Finally, videotaping is a private matter. Make a separate tape for each person, and let them take it home so they can use it to work on their skills.

Try videotaping at your next sales meeting, and make it a fun experience. If it's presented that way, it will be readily accepted by just about everyone. If it's presented in a negative way, those you are trying to help will resent the whole experience. But used properly, there's no better sales training tool.

31
Lead with gentleness and humility

ONE TRAIT I ADMIRE in people is gentleness. But in today's fast-paced world, words like *gentleness* and *thoughtfulness* are unlikely to come into play when the topic of leadership is discussed. Other skills seem to be more important: the ability to make decisions, the ability to read a financial statement, the ability to give direction to subordinates, and a lot of other things that by themselves are important but in many ways don't have a darn thing to do with leadership. That's because the art of leadership is a very special kind of discipline. Unfortunately, most leaders really don't understand it. But the problem is even more basic.

Individuals who are unsure of themselves have a tendency to bully. You've seen it, and so have I. It's a false bravado that manifests itself when undisciplined leaders can't think of anything else to do but push others around. They're stuck, because they haven't thought things through.

In other cases, they simply aren't sensitive to those around them, because they're so wrapped up in their own worlds. They feel everyone is against them. It's called insecurity. Too many companies still tolerate this kind of behavior, but in the future it's just not going to work.

Younger people today are better educated, more cynical, and less tolerant of baloney from so-called leaders who lack vision, don't understand the organization's mission, and are devoid of ethics. The young people entering the workplace are looking for enlightened leaders. And I also think they're more idealistic than they're given credit for. They're crying out for direction, but the disappointment is that too many people in leadership positions just don't know how to do the job.

What are the tenets of good leadership? It all starts with humility. By that I mean not overestimating your own role. Too many executives think their organizations would fall apart were it not for their talent and dedication. That may not be far from the truth in some cases, but wise leaders realize that if they and their organizations are to stay in business, they have to surround themselves with people who are just as talented and dedicated, if not more so. That's tough for many people. They don't want to share power, because, as I've indicated, they're too insecure about their own abilities.

Even more important is the desire to treat your colleagues and customers with a gentleness that inspires confidence and loyalty. For some people that's hard to do, because they feel vulnerable when they show their emotions. Others just don't know how to demonstrate kindness and thoughtfulness.

84

It's really quite simple, if you think about it. Remembering a colleague's birthday is a good start. Other thoughtful actions include writing a personal note to someone who's lost a loved one, or driving a friend home when he's under the weather. Or how about sending flowers to a couple on their anniversary, or picking up the phone to tell some longtime customers how much they mean to you?

It's all very easy, but it requires leaders to be with their people, not in some office on the top floor where there's no noise and no laughter and where everyone is afraid to say anything for fear of being criticized or ridiculed. Good leaders know where their people are and what they need, because they're good listeners.

Not very sophisticated stuff, but it makes a big difference in today's work environment. Go ahead and try it, but make sure you really care about your colleagues. They'll know if you're pretending.

32
The value of a messy desk

WE'VE ALL HEARD the clichés: You can tell a lot about a person by the way he plays golf. Or never trust someone who won't look you in the eye. You could probably add a few dozen more. All kinds of sayings offer insight into sizing people up. A messy desk is a sign of a disorganized mind, or something to that effect, is another one I've heard before. So at the end of each day, I try to clean up my desk to show at least some semblance of organization. But if you were to drop in on me during the workday, I'm afraid my desk would look somewhat like a trash heap.

My desk also seems to have secret compartments that swallow letters, memos, and other important documents. Papers mysteriously disappear from right under my nose. My secretary has caught on to this phenomenon and now will not leave anything on my

85

desk until she has made at least five or six copies. She does this because it's not unusual for two or three copies of something to vanish from my desktop. It's a perplexing problem. Someday I'm going to talk to the folks who supply office equipment about this matter.

On the other hand, after reading about some new research, maybe the untidy state of my desk isn't such a bad thing after all.

Some unusual findings came out of a study conducted by Jericho Promotions, based in New York. The firm surveyed 1,112 top executives at *Fortune* 1,000 companies. In short, the results would seem to indicate that the messier the executive's desk, the better. For instance, stocks of companies headed by executives with messy desks rose an average of 3.5 percent in one year, while stock prices of companies whose key executives kept their desks squeaky clean fell about 1 percent during the same period.

The study showed that 58 percent of the executives surveyed claimed they kept their desks spotless. (I wonder how that could be verified.) Another 31 percent said their desks were messy, and about 11 percent said theirs were somewhere in between. I think most of us would probably fit in the latter category.

Some other findings also were eye-openers. For instance, only about 16 percent of executives with tidy desks said they believed in giving employees Christmas bonuses, while 48 percent of those who owned up to having messy desks said they favored the bonuses.

Only 21 percent of the executives sitting behind neat desks said they were popular in high school, while 54 percent of those with messy desks said they were popular in their high school years.

Social consciousness came up too. Some 71 percent of execs with sloppy desks said they believed in affirmative action, while only about 21 percent of the tidy execs claimed they believed in such programs.

It's amazing what might be gleaned from simply looking at someone's desk. There doesn't seem to be any facet of our lives that isn't being put under a microscope and interpreted by re-searchers and pollsters. It's certainly interesting stuff, but we might be going a little too far. One of the side effects of this could be stereotyping, and that would be unfortunate. Remember that Homo sapiens are an unpredictable bunch. To try to categorize us by the cleanliness of our desks might be a stretch.

Then again, the next time your boss stops by, you might want to bring up the saying that a messy desk can mask a brilliant mind.

Avoiding black holes

33
Dangerous seductions of success

SUCCESS IS WONDERFUL. It's what we all strive for. It's the name of the game. When it happens, there's no other feeling like it. But success is also dangerous and seductive. In fact, when a company or organization achieves success, that's often when the seeds of failure are sown.

How many major corporations have we seen achieve success—then, in a very short time, abruptly start to unravel? This phenomenon, one of the great paradoxes of life, has always been something to fear, but most companies simply don't prepare for achieving success, because they're too preoccupied with getting there.

But let's first talk about successful organizations and how they got that way. Right off the bat, everyone knew the company's objectives. No one said, "I can't do that. It's not my job." Management didn't get all upset because some of the salespeople were making too much money. They were simply happy to see their products and services being sold to as many customers as possible. The goal of any organization at the beginning is as American as apple pie—to make money. Achieving that goal means everyone gets to keep their jobs. At the same time, everyone is expected to help everyone else. There's no room for egos. The only thing management should care about is getting more customers. That's the ultimate goal. Simple, isn't it? But how soon we forget.

Success can really screw things up. That's why leadership is so important at this stage. The person who runs the place must be on constant guard against anything that threatens to derail the organization's prosperity. Management should have the gumption to identify problems and then fix them—fast, before the failure disease spreads.

89

What are some of the negative manifestations of success? The word *complacency* comes to mind immediately. Understand that it's OK to pause briefly and take a deep breath, but in too many cases complacency becomes a habit and turns into arrogance. Arrogance is fatal.

Another warning sign is when customers are considered a bother and consequently are taken for granted. When customers call, they're thought of as an interruption. The organization thinks of ways to outwit its customers instead of understanding that customers should be considered partners and colleagues.

Then there's the tendency at these newly successful companies to build a bureaucracy. Suddenly more accountants appear on the scene as management becomes preoccupied with all the money the company is making, wanting to protect it not only from the tax collector but from the employees too.

All of this also is mixed with a little paranoia. More supervisors are appointed to oversee people who have more than proven their loyalty in helping the firm achieve success, but for some strange reason management now seems to believe these same individuals bear watching. That's when morale takes a nose dive.

At the same time, executives begin to pull away from the day-to-day activities of the company, because they now believe they need to spend less time managing and more time acting like "top executives." These so-called executives distance themselves from the very customers who have made them successful, by appointing regional managers or account managers to handle the clients.

Selling and spending time on the road visiting customers is just too inconvenient, especially with all the decisions that have to be made about that new headquarters building going up. The top concerns become things like deciding what kind of furniture to order or what brand of word processors to install or making sure the E-mail system is working smoothly. The top concern is no longer the customer who made everything happen. Not the customer who is being called on by competitors every day. Not the customer who constantly needs reassurances that you value his or her business. The worries now are things that have nothing to do with success. They're the worries of a company destined for hard times.

Laughter and spontaneity also begin to disappear at companies that aren't prepared for success. That's because members of management begin to take themselves too seriously and neglect the dedicated employees whose contributions made success possible. Saying thank you and giving people positive stroking is crucial for good morale.

Probably the most obvious sign of decay is when the lore of an organization begins to disappear. Those stories about this person or that person making a big sale or developing a new product or winning a prestigious award are important to the tradition of any successful enterprise. Keeping that history alive shows pride and a caring attitude about what made the organization a winner.

So, the point is this: Success, like anything else, has to be planned for. It can't be a last-minute thing. Those companies that simply "wing it" are in for some serious problems. It has to be taken as seriously as any other long-term strategy.

Success is great, but learning how to handle it is even greater. And that's really the only way to make sure your success will continue.

34
Warning signs
of an organization in trouble

AT A CEO CONFERENCE I attended, the head of a major health care supply house was recounting the reasons his company had enjoyed so much success. He was proud of the corporate culture he had been able to establish in only a few years, but as he related how his company had forged ahead, he also acknowledged that some negatives were beginning to creep into his organization—things he hadn't anticipated. He specifically mentioned internal politics and selfishness. Let me elaborate.

There are warning signs of decay in any organization. One is when politics starts playing a major role. People start jockeying for position so they can further their own careers. Some of the tactics they use are anything but ethical. But politics in any outfit is like a cancer. It's the job of the person at the top to attack the problem early, or it could be lethal.

Another caution signal is when individuals within a company start developing what I call a compartmentalization attitude. The symptoms are obvious. You hear things like, "My people can't do that. We're too busy with our own assignments" or, "I can't answer that phone. It's not my department." If these phenomena sound familiar, I'll bet your organization is headed in the wrong direction. Failure could be just around the corner.

Teamwork has to be the first order of the day. No matter where the telephone rings, it should be everyone's responsibility to answer it. No excuses.

If you want to stay successful, there should be a simple mission: getting and keeping customers. That's the only way to stay in business. And, while doing so, make sure everyone is treated with dignity and respect. It's crucial that employees be given the latitude to do their jobs the best way they know how.

Selling always comes to mind when I talk about these things. Too many salespeople are literally prohibited from doing their jobs because of bureaucratic rules and regulations. It's done because managers may be afraid they'll lose control if they don't let everyone know who's the boss. Salespeople need room. They're creative types who, treated properly, will make your outfit successful beyond your wildest dreams.

Finally, keep the organization focused. Companies that stay successful do one or two things right. They don't complicate the mission by going off in too many directions. It only confuses your people and dilutes their energies. Invest your company's financial and human capital in the core business.

In short, never forget how you got where you are. And remember who got you there.

35

The death star: Complacency

COMPLACENCY IS SOMETHING to be feared by anyone in business. It's an easy trap to fall into, and once you do, it's the kiss of death. I've seen companies suffering from a bad case of complacency-itis, and management usually doesn't have the slightest idea what's going on.

I addressed this topic briefly on page 90, but it merits further consideration. Complacency should serve as a wake-up call. Most often, it strikes at organizations that have been highly successful and have fought tooth and nail to get where they are. But for some reason, after they've risen to the top and have stayed there for some time, they enter into a trance and seemingly forget everything. Tragically, they even forget why they're in business and consequently forget to do what's necessary to stay on top. The most telling indictment is when the customers start to suffer.

Now, don't think complacency is found only at top companies. I've encountered marginal businesses with complacency written all over them. Staff at these organizations do only what they have to do to get by and nothing more. That's why their companies will never go on to bigger and better things. People at the top don't provide leadership. They don't get down in the trenches and communicate the company's mission, vision, and values.

Yes, complacency can infect any business, but it *always* happens when an organization has enjoyed some measure of success. That's why an article by Mark McCormack in *Incentive* magazine caught my attention.

93

Mr. McCormack is chairman of the International Management Group, a Cleveland-based sports marketing firm, and author of *What They Don't Teach You at Harvard Business School* (Bantam, 1984) and its sequel, *What They Still Don't Teach You at Harvard Business School* (Bantam, 1990). He basically preaches common sense in both books. If you're a leader, the books will give you plenty of advice on how to run your organization successfully. His article, titled "Don't Play Games With Your Customers," offers more invaluable advice.

Mr. McCormack offers some danger signs to heed before you or your colleagues get to the crisis stage with an account. Most of them are minor things, but they can become dangerously critical. If you don't have your antennae up, they can be missed.

Here are some to watch for:

■ You're too busy to return a client's calls promptly.

■ You schedule meetings at your convenience rather than the customer's.

■ You lie to a client rather than admit that you were wrong or that you just don't know.

■ You send an associate in your place and don't explain why.

■ You don't think it affects you when the client puts a new person in charge.

■ You knowingly do less than your best, yet you expect the client to give you the benefit of the doubt.

■ You hear that the client is being wooed by your competition, but you fail to confront the issue.

That's quite a checklist. While none of those things may stand out as a bell ringer, any one of them could spell disaster.

There are other warning signs. Some are obvious. One indication of trouble is when key managers worry more about the titles and power they have than about the future success of the business. In short, these people are more concerned about their careers than they are about their company's prosperity.

Another sign of impending danger is starting to think of the client as a bother or making fun of the client to your colleagues. I've even heard a salesperson call one of her customers a four-letter word because the client's actions didn't fit her idea of how that client should be doing business with her. This was a client who over the years had given her hundreds of thousands of dollars worth of business.

Those of us in sales know how disastrous complacency can be. It happens all the time. A salesperson sells an account, services that account for a few years, but then begins to take that account very much for granted. He or she doesn't go to see the client more than once a year, doesn't return telephone calls right away, and forgets to do the little things that are essential to keeping an account sold. Then, seemingly all of a sudden, it happens. The account goes to a competitor. No warning, simply a loss of business and a loss of commissions. Then the furtive phone call. What happened? What did I do wrong? What do I have to do to get the business back? Once you lose an account, it usually takes a long time to get it back—if you ever do.

It's amazing how comfortable we become. It's amazing how short our memories are concerning all the blood, sweat, and tears it took to land a certain account. Then it disappears overnight just because we couldn't be bothered.

Complacency masks arrogance, and arrogance spells failure. Show me an arrogant salesperson or manager, and I'll show you a loser. Quality people have plenty of humility. They listen well, they dote on their customers, and they're worried all the time that they haven't done enough for their clients. The one thing that never enters their minds is complacency. That's because they love success, and taking care of the customer is the surest route to that success.

What's my advice? Stay in touch with your clients all the time! No matter what the new breed of consultants say and what some of the new breed of managers say, stay in touch by making calls face to face, eyeball to eyeball. That's the best way to service an account and keep it forever. There is simply no easy way.

Finally, never take anything for granted. Always be on your toes, and always make sure you're listening to your customers. They're the lifeblood of any organization and are hard to replace once you lose them.

36

Taste the nectar of success: Master ambiguity

ON A TRIP to St. Louis to visit one of our clients, I had the pleasure of lunching with the company's chief executive and two of his key colleagues. The CEO is someone I have admired for some time, not only because of his knowledge of what's going on in his field but also because of his management style. He appears to be quite comfortable with all the change and ambiguity that most of us struggle with on a day-to-day basis. As we chatted, he made this comment: "What all of us are looking for are individuals who can deal with ambiguity, and we're having a tough time finding them." That particular observation didn't really register with me at the time, but as I thought about it, the statement made more and more sense.

The genius of any leader is the ability to anticipate change and prepare his or her company for the anxiety that can come with it. Today, everything seems to be on the table. It's an uncertainty that's causing a lot of people to do something they wouldn't ordinarily do—make poor decisions. This isn't anything we haven't all seen, but it's still startling when you observe it.

With that in mind, I thought it would be a good idea to look up the meaning of the word *ambiguous*. According to the *American Heritage Dictionary*, Second College Edition, it's defined as: 1. Susceptible to multiple interpretations. 2. Doubtful or uncertain.

In other words, it means things are not only confusing but in a sense are up for grabs. That isn't necessarily the way a college professor or even a management consultant might see it, but that's what the term conveys to me.

What's the point? With all the change that's taking place, it's incumbent upon all of us to have a core plan that we can stick with no matter what happens. However, it also means we have to be prepared to alter our thinking, if necessary, when something over which we have no control suddenly surfaces.

One key word is *flexibility.* Another is *courage.* Maybe that's why so many young people aren't interested in pursuing leadership positions. They simply don't want to take the heat and assume the responsibility for other people. Leadership requires individuals who enjoy the challenges of ambiguity and find nothing but opportunity in changing times. In my lifetime I've met some great leaders, and the one thing they had in common was an enthusiastic ability to deal with change. I could almost say they craved it, because they recognized the potential for growth.

So it was a simple statement over lunch by an individual I respect that got me thinking about what it's going to take to prosper during the next few years. Being able to separate the fluff from the real stuff is an integral part of it. There are a lot of glitzy fads out there right now, and too many of us are getting caught up in them. But they never last. Yes, these are confusing times, but fundamental principles still apply—things like sticking to the basics of your business.

Sticking to what you know best and keeping things simple is a formula all of us should keep in mind. It's one sure way to deal with ambiguity. But don't be a stick-in-the-mud if opportunities come along that are yours for the taking. Be aggressive and creative, always remembering that if the needs of the customer come first, you can't go too far off track.

To those who like being involved and enjoy their work, ambiguity is the nectar of success. The pros anticipate change and turn it to their advantage. The amateurs either run from it or freeze in their tracks; therefore they lose—and lose big. Go with the pros.

97

37

Professionals change for the right reasons

IT'S TOUGH TO BE a professional these days. By professionals, I mean the unsung individuals who go about their business in a competent manner day in and day out. It's routine stuff, really, and not too glamorous. Professionals don't make a big deal out of their competence. Unfortunately, because of their demeanor, they can be overlooked, when their attributes and performance really should be exalted as the standard.

Reliability, trustworthiness, and high ethical standards also are marks of a professional, but too often it's the flash-in-the-pan or the person with the advanced degree who gets the promotion or new title.

Amateurs are easy to recognize. They're the ones always in a hurry to make changes and get something done. For them, change is a sign of being dynamic and decisive. Thinking things through and making decisions based on solid data doesn't seem to fit their style. Change is effective and appropriate when planned and well thought out, but change for change's sake can be both destructive and tragic.

Look around, and you'll see it happening. Say a company names a new CEO. What's the first thing the so-called dynamic executive does? He or she immediately starts to make changes. In some cases, the changes are necessary, but in other cases, it's simply a way to show everyone that a boss has arrived who's willing to take risks with other people's careers. The words used are *downsizing* and *right sizing*. It looks great to the outside world when the justification is a leaner and meaner organization, but

98

that's not always the case. Too often, soon after some wizard has been brought in to turn things around, the wizard is let go when the changes he or she initiated end up destroying the company's morale. The successor is usually left with a big mess.

A question we have to keep asking ourselves is: Are we changing for change's sake, or are we taking the time to make decisions based on the facts? There seems to be a pervasive mentality that we'd better act before it's too late. Maybe that's legitimate. Maybe not. Professionals study the data and then take action. Amateurs don't pause and consider the alternatives. They simply act because it means they're doing something.

No doubt about it—in today's get-things-done environment, it's hard to be a professional.

38
Winners don't hold grudges

I DON'T THINK BUSINESS SCHOOLS teach it, and I haven't seen it mentioned in any of the management books I've read. I'm talking about learning to let go of those destructive grudges. It seems so fundamental, yet all the time I talk to people who keep hanging on to experiences long after they were apparently wronged.

You've probably witnessed it yourself. How many times have you interviewed someone for a job, and the person immediately starts talking about how badly he or she was treated by previous employers? Most of us really don't care about what went on in someone's previous position unless it happens to affect the person's qualifications for the new job, but that's usually not the case.

A few years ago, a young man came to see me about a sales job. This individual looked terrific on paper. When I met him, he greeted me with a firm handshake and good eye contact. From all appearances, he was an outstanding candidate. But it wasn't long into the interview before this person proceeded to tell me what a bunch of crooks his previous bosses had been. He wouldn't—and couldn't—stop, and he really turned me off.

I'm not saying a little anger isn't a great motivator. It is, and it works wonders when you're trying to outsell a competitor. You just can't let it consume you. That kind of thinking can lead to all kinds of stupid behavior. The healthy brand of anger, on the other hand, is a fleeting thing. You blow off a little steam and then get on with your life. But keeping those grudges alive is something that saps your joy and energy and only leads to disappointment and failure. Getting even becomes an almost daily preoccupation and breeds negative thinking.

Many of the top executives I have met seem to be able to get on with their lives without holding grudges and harboring animosity against those who supposedly have done them wrong. They just don't waste their time worrying about these things. But too many individuals do. They want to get revenge. They want to even the score with this person or that company and make them pay, no matter what the cost.

My advice? Give it up! Throw that kind of thinking out the window. It isn't going to do you or your career any good. Let's face it. We've all had raw deals. We've all had someone say something that wasn't true and hurt our feelings.

Instead of holding grudges, winners end up forgiving those who've hurt them the most. I've seen it so many times and have always marveled at the character of those who are able to conduct themselves in such a manner. They show their class by rising above petty grudges. Those are the kinds of leaders we all look up to, because they lead by example.

Leaders remember that they represent the interests of the entire organization, not just themselves. They know that when a grudge or some other selfish act comes into play, it can jeopardize the well-being of everyone involved. Simply put, true leaders don't let selfish motives allow them to take their eyes off the ball.

To me, part of growing up is learning to forgive those who've hurt you, whether they've fired you, ignored you, insulted you, or rejected you. The important thing is to get on with your life. But if you're living in the past, holding grudges, losing sleep, and boring everybody with your tales of woe, you really aren't going anywhere. You're standing still, and that's a tragedy. Don't fall into that trap. Grudges are for losers. Learn to forgive and forget.

39
You asked for it, or, Don't penalize candor

CANDOR IS A WONDERFUL THING when employed properly, but it can backfire if used incorrectly. That came to mind when I read an article in the *Wall Street Journal* about leveling with the boss when you're asked to give an appraisal of his or her performance on the job.

Bosses are no different from anyone else. They want to know what others think of the job they're doing. It's no secret they have the same insecurities that plague all of us, but beware if you're ever put on the spot and asked for your candid opinion. It could be a career-threatening event. At least that's what we're told in the article by Dee Soder, identified as president of Endymion Executive Assessments and Advisory Services in New York.

Here's what Ms. Soder says about bosses who ask for feedback: "A lot of times, they really don't want it." She then describes what happened to one executive at a Midwestern bank who made the mistake of being forthright. One evening while the executive and his boss were having a few drinks, the boss asked why two of the executive's colleagues had quit. Thinking of the boss more as a friend, the executive gave him the straight stuff. The two colleagues had quit because they wanted more pay and didn't like the boss's management style. The executive thought his candor would curry favor with his superior, but two weeks later he was demoted.

Ms. Soder explains that before you criticize your boss, it's best to question your own motives first. "If it's to nail him, then keep your mouth shut," Ms. Soder urges.

Peller Marion, an executive coach and outplacement counselor in San Francisco, shed more light on this type of office dilemma. According to the *Journal* article, he claims that if you really think changes need to be made, you should first assess how much "credit you have in the bank with your boss." In short, if your work record is above average, you're probably on safer ground, but it's still risky business.

Bosses must be prepared to be surprised, maybe even startled, when they ask colleagues to be honest with them about the state of affairs in the office. Mr. Marion reminds bosses that they must be prepared for any eventuality when they ask for candor—and never should they overreact.

He talks about a boss at a medium-sized company who called together some employees for a brown-bag lunch. The company had gone through a tough downsizing, so he wanted to get some feedback on morale at the firm. When he heard that morale was low, he responded: "I guess you're right. I guess I'm the bad guy in these downsizings." Other employees heard about the session, and when they were invited to subsequent meetings, they simply kept their mouths shut. Because nobody said anything, "the boss thought everything was fine," Mr. Marion said. He had shut down the line of communication with his employees by his self-pitying remarks.

Why is this so important? Because in today's work environment, there must be candid communication between leaders and their colleagues. Leaders with tin ears only deceive and shortchange themselves and the companies they work for. True leaders listen to those around them and, when appropriate, follow advice. That's how organizations grow. Penalizing people for their candor only breeds insecurity and unhappiness. Good people will leave any environment like that to find a more enlightened workplace.

It all boils down to leadership. Every industry needs to

develop leaders who have enough confidence in themselves that no matter what they are told, they react in a positive and measured manner. It's a commonsense approach to management, and it usually foretells how successful a company is going to be.

40
Another star destroyer: Failure to provide training and support

I'D LIKE TO SHARE a couple of stories about two young women who wanted to get into sales. Both succeeded in getting jobs rather quickly. However, after only brief stints, they're both out of the business, at least temporarily. In both cases, problems with leadership and training were to blame. It bothers me to see this kind of thing happen. Unfortunately, it's not an uncommon occurrence.

The first story involves a woman who was an executive secretary. She's bright, energetic, and full of enthusiasm. She talked to me about getting into sales, and I urged her to give it a try. I talked to her about the travel, rejection, and all the other things she could expect as she began her new career. It didn't take long for her to land a job with a young, aggressive company in the electronics field. It looked like a good deal. She was told she would have to relocate from her home, but she was looking forward to the move and couldn't wait to get started. I was excited for her, because she had all the attributes necessary for success.

The week before she was to begin, she had lunch with the fellow who would be her supervisor. He told her, among other things, that they would spend her first week in the field making calls. She phoned to tell me this, and I wished her luck and told her

103

to keep me posted. Almost ten days passed before I heard from her again. But by then she had already resigned from her new job.

It took me a while to get the story out of her, but I learned what triggered her decision to quit. It occurred when she and her new boss were dining with a client. The boss apparently felt compelled to tell an off-color story and asked her to leave the table until he finished. Imagine treating a twenty-five-year-old woman like a little girl and embarrassing her in front of a client. That happened the second night out on the inaugural trip for the sales rookie. From there, things went from bad to worse.

The second story is a little different. This young woman had always wanted to get into textbook sales. She's in her late twenties and had been employed as a physical therapist. She's also very talented and has plenty of determination. She finally made up her mind to pursue a job in sales, so she sent her résumé to a number of publishers. She quickly landed a job and was very excited.

For the first couple of months, she was on the road almost constantly. It was grueling, and her supervisor was absent virtually the whole time. She became discouraged and depressed, and she too resigned. Later she told me that aside from the fact that she didn't like the heavy travel, there just wasn't anyone she could talk to. She ended up feeling lost and thought nobody cared.

Here are two very capable individuals who were eager to jump into new careers. But because their employers offered poor training and incompetent leadership, they've lost interest in their chosen field—at least for the time being. I hear too many stories like these.

When someone is hired, no matter what the job or the company, he or she must be given the courtesy of adequate training and supervision. That's only fair and proper.

Furthermore, those who will be training and managing others should themselves be thoroughly screened and trained. That's why leadership training is a must. Having supervisory power is a heavy responsibility, and those who abuse that privilege must be reprimanded or even terminated.

Sure, it's a tough world out there, but it shouldn't be made any tougher just because those in positions of leadership don't have what it takes to do the job.

41

Guidelines for judging who deserves a promotion

THERE ARE CERTAIN WAYS to gain advancement and promotion. One is by doing it the old-fashioned way. Get to work on time, do your job right day in and day out, keep your nose clean and remain loyal to your employer. At most companies, that kind of performance pays off—but we all know it isn't always that simple. There's usually politics involved. You cater to the boss. You listen to every word he or she has to say and, to the best of your abilities, try to do what he or she wants. Sometimes you disagree, but you still go ahead and do what's expected of you and you keep your mouth shut.

Of course, there's another way to gain advancement, and that's by being born into the family business. For these lucky folks, promotions usually come fast, and the wear and tear isn't quite as bad as it can be for the rest of us. Ironically, many people who inherit the family business don't want to work as hard as the old man did, so they simply sell out and do other things.

Then there are the slick operators who don't let ethics, loyalty, or basic decency get in the way of upward mobility. These individuals are usually easy to spot because of their blind ambition. But in their own minds, surprisingly, they feel they're going about their career-climbing without anyone noticing what's going on. That's because of their egos and lack of sensitivity. But these climbers share plenty of other telltale traits.

The first thing they usually do is attempt to create as much turmoil as they possibly can. They love to bring about what I call *manufactured crises*. Everything has to be done now, which usually keeps everyone off balance and very ill at ease. They like to give the impression that everything is urgent.

These types are often very smart and have great energy, but they're also loose cannons who can be quite destructive if left unattended. They act as though they know everything about everything, even when they don't have any actual experience. To these people, nothing is ever right. They can't stand to see things running smoothly. They always find fault, because they want others to think they could do better. Arrogance is not foreign to them.

But the trait that really shines through is the lack of sensitivity toward others. They're so wrapped up with their own career paths and ambitions that they don't care what happens to others. They put on great performances about how much they care, and, tragically, they often have responsibility for supervising others. But they really don't care, and that becomes obvious to all who report to them. These people don't listen, and they don't go out of their way to help others. More often than not, they do go out of their way to destroy the careers and good reputations of others.

Also, most of them want titles. They feel titles give them power, and that's what they're really after—power over other people's lives. They want money, too, but give them a choice between a title and money...and they'll usually take the title.

So, if you have a business to run, be careful. Reward people who are truly loyal and care about others. They might be plodders, but they get the job done, and they won't jump at the first chance to go over to a competitor because someone offered a bigger title and more power. If you are a boss, be careful with people who crave power, because someday they might bring you down too. By promoting such people, you often destroy your own career.

If you identify people in your organization with these traits, it's a good idea to pay close attention to their behavior and see if there's some way to bring them around. It won't be easy and, in some cases, it will be impossible. However, in the long run, if you can get them to channel their energy into positive, constructive, and creative enterprises, then you will have helped your company and made a major contribution to someone's career. In itself, that is worth a try.

Profiles in management and leadership excellence

42

Profile of Chip Chapman: Respect for others personified

 ERIE "CHIP" CHAPMAN is an individual who has made a difference. He epitomizes the very best in enlightened management. He's a doer, a man who knows how to get things accomplished. He breaks with tradition and, in doing so, sometimes gets people upset. But that's the penalty of leadership. Leaders don't wait for others to catch up; they go out and do it. That kind of leadership isn't for the meek, because it involves a lot of stress.

First in the hospital industry and now at InPhyNet, Chip Chapman has done a first-rate job. His philosophy is simple. First of all, he realizes that management doesn't take care of people; front-line staff people do. So he reasons that if he and his colleagues in management take good care of employees, then those employees will probably do a better job of taking care of the patients and their families. It's called empowering your people and treating them with dignity and respect.

So what's so special about the way Mr. Chapman handles day-to-day activities? Let me give you a few examples of the kinds of things he did when he was president and CEO of a hospital group. First of all, only about one hundred feet from the main hospital building at one of the hospitals is a day care center that can handle as many as 240 kids. That takes a lot of stress and worry out of the lives of parents who work at the hospital.

This hospital also has an employee convenience center that offers shoe repair, video rental, dry cleaning, and a grocery shopping service. For instance, an employee who begins work at 6:30 A.M. can drop off an order in the morning and pick up the groceries on the way home in the afternoon. Often, when Chip Chapman walked the halls of the hospital, a nurse or other employee would grab him by the arm and tell him how much of a lifesaver the center had been.

Then there was the employee-recognition event—with a twist. Instead of a routine banquet, Mr. Chapman and his colleagues decided to bring in some "name" entertainment such as Doc Severinsen, Dionne Warwick, and Barbara Mandrell. Mr. Chapman felt this was one way to show thousands of employees how much they were valued.

Furthermore, this hospital started calling its workers *partners* rather than employees. "It's the essence of our concept of management," Mr. Chapman said, when this practice began. "We don't work for each other, we work with each other."

And how about this one: Mr. Chapman had a wardrobe of eighteen different hospital uniforms. About once a month, he worked a shift in the laundry service, housekeeping, or any other department. He didn't go there for a photo opportunity; he actually worked a shift. His only goal was to show his people he was with them.

The "living memorial" program at the hospital was also unique. Employees always have suggestions, but at the hospital, if an employee suggested something and action was taken as a result, the person's name was actually placed on the stamp machine, drinking fountain, or whatever else the employee suggested. Again, think how important that must make the partners feel.

That's leadership, and that's smart.

Chip Chapman continues to do the same kinds of things at InPhyNet. It's simple, really. He excels because he has two important qualities—common sense and respect for others. And when you come right down to it, that's what leadership basically is.

43
Profile of Betina Echols: Rewarding the good people

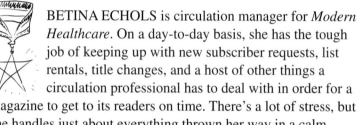

BETINA ECHOLS is circulation manager for *Modern Healthcare*. On a day-to-day basis, she has the tough job of keeping up with new subscriber requests, list rentals, title changes, and a host of other things a circulation professional has to deal with in order for a magazine to get to its readers on time. There's a lot of stress, but she handles just about everything thrown her way in a calm manner. However, just to make sure everything keeps running smoothly, a few months ago we initiated a system whereby every few weeks Echols personally briefs me, our editor, and our national sales director on any problems or developments in the circulation department. So far, it's worked very well. But something happened recently that I consider remarkable.

Echols was updating us on a variety of matters, when she brought up the extra duties one employee was handling in the department that makes sure the mailing addresses of *Modern Healthcare*'s readers are up to date. She named the person and proceeded to tell us how this individual, because of the department's heavy workload, had been taking work home on weeknights and weekends. Then Echols said something that immediately caught my attention. She didn't make a big deal out of it, but was I impressed.

Because of all the extra work the clerk was doing, Echols took it upon herself to give the employee a frequent flier ticket she had earned from one of the major airlines. I asked her why she had done this, and she said it was simply her way of rewarding a colleague who had gone out of her way to do a better job. Now

110

that's what I would have to call going above and beyond the call of duty.

I asked Echols how many free tickets she had stashed away from all the trips she took on that airline. She said that was the only one, but she was happy to give it to her colleague. I was so proud of Echols that I stopped the meeting to tell her how inspiring that story was to me. I also told her she had the one quality most effective leaders possess: thinking about the needs of their employees. In too many cases leaders forget to reward good people. They worry more about themselves and their own rewards than they do about those who toil in the trenches doing the work that needs to get done if a business is going to flourish.

Effective leaders are always on the lookout for people who go the extra mile. And when they find them, they reward them. It might be a handwritten note, a plant, or a couple of tickets to a ball game. Whatever it is, it's a token of appreciation for a job well done. In my eyes, people who go out of their way to show they care about their charges are big-time managers.

We all know bosses who think this is a bunch of bull. Their reasoning is simplistic. They believe that the person is already getting paid and is expected to do a good job. So why go any further? But it shouldn't take a genius to figure out why. When the boss goes out of his or her way to thank an employee who has done exceptional work, it shows that the boss cares. And that can send morale sky high. Some studies even indicate that this kind of reward does more for a person's morale than a raise.

Betina Echols, you made my day by being the thoughtful person you are. You shouldn't have any trouble with your future at all. That's because you've got a winning attitude, and it's contagious.

44

Profile of Southwest Airlines: Treating employees with respect

 THE IDEA OF TREATING your colleagues like customers isn't a new concept, but I became fascinated with the philosophy as I read two articles on the workings of Dallas-based Southwest Airlines. One appeared in *Conomikes Reports*, a newsletter that covers medical practice management and managed care. The newsletter often takes a look at other industries to see what lessons can be adapted to health care. The other article was in the *Wall Street Journal*. Both give solid testimony to why Southwest is one of the most successful airlines in the country, and both offer insights valuable for any organization.

The *Conomikes* article touched on the way Southwest hires people. You may or may not know that, according to one analysis, Southwest ranks among the ten best companies to work for in America. One of the key reasons is the carrier's hiring practices. "What we are looking for first and foremost is a sense of humor," Herbert Kelleher, Southwest's chairman and CEO, told *Fortune* magazine. "Then we're looking for people who have to excel to satisfy themselves and who work well in a collegial environment. We don't care much about education and experience, because we can train people to do whatever they have to do. We hire attitudes."

As an addendum to his statement, the newsletter states that the airline looks for "listening, caring, smiling, polite and warm" people, whether they're flight attendants or staff in the accounting department.

With such criteria, it's no wonder the airline is doing so well. You've heard me say it before, and I'll say it again: Attitude is everything. I don't care how much education or experience you have—if you don't have a good attitude about yourself and your company, you're in trouble. And humor is important in any work environment. It all adds up to healthy morale.

The *Wall Street Journal* article highlights the contributions of Colleen Barrett to the success of Southwest. Based on what I read, she embodies the spirit of the airline. According to Kevin Freiberg, president of San Diego Consulting Group, which has worked with Southwest for some twelve years, "If Kelleher is the brains of the business, [Barrett] is the heart."

Barrett started out as Kelleher's legal secretary at a San Antonio law firm in 1967. In the early '70s, she and Kelleher took leaves of absence from the firm to help the fledgling airline. In 1981 they both came on board full time with Southwest. Barrett has risen to executive vice president of customers and corporate secretaries. As Kelleher's de facto chief of staff, she executes policies, oversees hiring and firing, and, in a very real sense, sets the agenda for the airline.

Her philosophy is quite simple: She doesn't believe in rigid and demeaning centralized policies. She believes employees should be treated like customers, and she's constantly on the lookout for workers who go above and beyond the call of duty. When she finds them, she makes sure their pursuit of excellence is rewarded.

Furthermore, Southwest employees are well paid compared with employees of other airlines. Barrett's philosophy is that building loyalty is crucially important to the success of the company. It's apparent that she also believes in empowerment and in treating each employee with dignity and respect.

That formula spells success for any organization, but too many so-called corporate leaders still don't get it. They're so concerned with the short-term bottom line that they forget that the long-term success of any business requires high-quality employees who love doing their jobs.

Southwest Airlines should be congratulated for such a common-sense approach to business. With that kind of attitude, no wonder Colleen Barrett and boss Herb Kelleher have become legends in the cutthroat airline industry. They're a winning combination.

Reaching the customer:

SUCCESS IN

SALES AND MARKETING

. . . .

"Most customers will give a salesperson
all the ammunition needed to make the sale.
But too often the salesperson is so intent
on making the sale that he or she isn't alert to
what the customer is trying to say."

*E*FFECTIVE *salespeople are perhaps the greatest students of human nature on the planet. They must know what makes people tick. They must know how to motivate people—to target those "hot buttons" that move them to a decision.*

Successful salespeople know how to listen, how to persuade, how to treat people with tact and respect, and—yes—how to ask for the sale. Selling is an honorable enterprise, and those who sell perform one of the world's greatest and most-needed services.

Qualities
for
success in sales

45

How to enter this most honorable profession

TO ME, SELLING is one of the most honorable professions there is. I don't care how good a product is or how bright a management team is—without sales-people, nothing happens. Look at most successful companies, and behind their triumphs you'll find a top-flight sales group. They make everything happen. They're the foot soldiers, the dreamers, the problem solvers.

Unfortunately, their eternal optimism often is misunderstood by their own colleagues in the home office, usually because those people don't understand what it's like to be in the trenches. Many of those people have never had to face the rejection, hard knocks, and hassles all salespeople endure every day. Too often, a lot of those hard knocks and bruises are inflicted by their own col-leagues and managers. That should never happen, but it's the reality of being in sales.

Selling is a tough business. There's no doubt about it. Today, you would think that anybody who wanted to get into sales would have the basics down pat. You would think even recent college graduates would at least have a passing knowledge of how to interview for a sales position. Believe me, that isn't the case. Far from it. Frankly, some of the young people I interview seem to want to get into sales simply because there isn't anything else available in the job market, and it would tide them over until something better comes along. The problem is, their lack of commitment and resolve becomes all too apparent only a few minutes into the interview.

Others, however, sincerely want a career in sales, and they're

118

the ones I like to talk to. And some of them really make an impression. You can't help but see it and feel it. You just know they'll do well.

Successful salespeople pay close attention to the fundamentals. For example, they always have calling cards with them. When they visit a company, they offer their credentials to the receptionist so she doesn't have to stumble around with spelling their name and the name of the company they represent.

Successful salespeople look organized. When they visit a client or prospect, they listen more than they talk. They listen to the customer's problems and needs, and they listen for new product ideas. You'd be surprised what you can learn when you really concentrate and listen.

Top salespeople also exude humility. They're always talking to colleagues and learning from them. And they look to their bosses for help and advice. In other words, they use all the resources available within their organizations to make a sale. Bringing their bosses along to close a sale or make a good impression on an important potential client is something that seems to be a common practice with the top performers in sales.

Those are just a few of the fundamentals. I also believe there are some basic characteristics and traits that are inherent in all successful salespeople. Consequently, I've put together seven recommendations that will help sales candidates demonstrate during a job interview that they have what it takes:

1. **Dress neatly and conservatively.** This is crucial, because how you groom yourself is the first thing an interviewer will notice. Don't wear loud clothes or dress like a rock star. It just doesn't make a good first impression. The interviewer is looking for a team player, not a maverick.

2. **Always, but always, look the interviewer in the eye.** I can't stress this enough. Too many people I interview can't look me in the eye for one or two seconds before they look to the floor or the wall. It shows a lack of concentration, and it's one of the biggest sins you can commit during the interviewing process.

3. **Always address the interviewer as ma'am or sir, whatever the case may be.** It's just good manners. Don't be glib and

casual. Remember, everything you say and do is being recorded in the interviewer's mental notebook. Smart alecks don't get jobs, because they make people uncomfortable.

4. **When you're asked why you want to get into sales, don't be afraid to tell the interviewer you want to make lots of money.** That's what sales is all about. It's as simple as that. Top salespeople love to make money, and they're willing to put up with all of the heartaches and rejection day after day to make their quotas and earn their commissions.

5. **Don't be afraid to tell the interviewer you like to work— and to work hard.** Pledge to give the company 100 percent every day. Don't be ashamed to say that, because it's what companies expect from positive-thinking sales candidates. However, sometimes people feel they're degrading themselves when they say such things. Say it, and say it again. Interviewers love to hear it.

6. **In everything you do, be enthusiastic and positive.** You can do this without being a phony. Make the interviewer think he or she is the most important person you've ever met.

7. **Lastly, use good common sense.** That's the best way to show your intelligence and maturity.

Finally, and most important, the stars in sales know what their job is all about—getting out in the field and selling—and they love doing it. But they know they must pay the price of discipline, organization, and team play.

The best salespeople I know are consummate team players because they not only enjoy their profession, but they're proud of their colleagues and the organizations they work for.

46
Ten absolute musts for sales success

 A FEW YEARS AGO, one of my top producers said she was having a problem with her personal sales calls. When I asked her what she meant, she told me she wasn't quite sure but that when she made her calls, something wasn't clicking. To help her pinpoint the problem, I went along on her next trip. We started by calling on an account executive at an advertising agency, and, right off the bat, it became clear why she was having problems. After going through the normal greetings, my sales star started her pitch before she even sat down—before any of us had the chance to sit down. When that happens, nine times out of ten things don't go very well.

Why? First of all, no salesperson should start talking until the customer has had a chance to speak first. Opening with something like, "Before I begin my presentation, do you have any questions?" gives the client the opportunity to speak. It's simply the polite thing to do and gives the salesperson a fix not only on what kind of mood the customer is in but also what things may be bothering him or her.

Second, there's the problem of ego. In their enthusiasm, salespeople sometimes forget when they're on a sales call that they're guests in someone else's domain. So we're really talking about good manners.

Remember that people like to be treated with dignity and respect, just like you and me, and when somebody breaks the basic tenets of good manners and professionalism, it creates barriers to effective communication and effective salesmanship. It's common sense, but too many people in sales fall into bad habits when they're left unsupervised. That was the problem with my employee, who sensed she was doing something wrong but couldn't put her finger on it. That's why it's so important for sales managers to get out with their people to make sure those bad habits never develop. Sure, it's time-consuming and inconvenient, but salespeople need to be monitored. The good ones will even welcome it.

I've developed some basic rules I feel are important in the selling process that I'd like to share with you. They're basic guidelines I've developed over the years, and I hope they'll be helpful to you in your efforts.

1. **Keep the focus where it belongs.** The product or service is the star of the show, not you. Too often I find that salespeople want to make a statement about themselves by the clothes they wear. That's not the purpose of the sales call. Everything should point up the strengths of what you're trying to sell.
2. **Bathe or shower at least once a day.** Cleanliness and a neat appearance go hand in hand, and it shows respect for the people you're calling on.
3. **Practice your sales pitch in front of a mirror.** As in everything else, practicing your pitch will improve your performance.
4. **Be brief.** Brevity will get you in the door again and again.
5. **Smile.** It's contagious.
6. **Never fail to ask for the order.** Conversely, always say thank you after you get the order.
7. **When you entertain, remember who you're entertaining.** Your focus should be on entertaining your client, not yourself.
8. **Be early for every call.** If you know you're going to be late, call ahead so your client isn't left waiting.
9. **Observe good manners.** Ladies and gentlemen stand out.
10. **Use a firm handshake.** It communicates sincerity, respect, and confidence.

Those are only ten of what I consider absolute musts for salespeople. There are a lot more, but what it all boils down to is this: Selling is basically good manners and common sense. There really isn't any mystery. When you read some of the books on the subject, you almost get the impression that there's some other dimension to it, but there isn't.

Then again, all the stuff that's been written about sales and all the advice that any of us give isn't worth a plug nickel unless the salesperson gets out and makes personal calls on customers. That's the key right there.

As a matter of fact, if you simply make personal calls and say each time, "You don't want to buy anything from me, do you?" you'll probably still do all right. You won't set any records, but you'll make a sale every once in a while. That's how much opportunity there is out there. And if you're willing to develop your sales skills to their fullest, there's absolutely no reason why success won't come your way.

47
See the people!

 I READ A VARIETY of sales publications to get ideas and to recharge my batteries. Sales, of course, is my first love, so reading about the trials and tribulations of salespeople is something I find fascinating. Selling is a tough way to make a living, and it's certainly not for everyone. It's a field filled with all kinds of adversity and uncertainty, but if one is willing to give every day 100 percent and take risks, there's no more rewarding way to fulfill one's destiny.

There's something even more basic about sales, however, that many people in the field still don't quite grasp. That's why I found a story in *Sales Upbeat*, published by Economics Press, to be so appropriate.

A number of years ago, a young man applied for a job at the International Shoe Co. The interviewer asked him the standard

123

question: "What can you do?" The earnest young man's reply was simple and honest: "I can farm. That's what I've been helping my dad with the last five years." Obviously, that reply didn't seem to make him too promising for the shoe business, but the recruiter continued the interview and became increasingly impressed with the man's sincerity. As a matter of fact, he was so impressed that he brought him into the company's sales trainee program.

The man must have worked very hard, because some years later he was named salesman of the year at International Shoe. Of course, as these things go, one night there was a dinner held in his honor. After dinner, the man was asked to say a few words. But when he got up to speak, he became tongue-tied and could only blurt out: "See the people! See the people! See the people!" Then he walked off the stage.

According to the story, the audience sat stunned for a few seconds, but after they realized the wisdom of what the young man had said, they gave him a standing ovation. It had dawned on them that the former farm boy had just summed up the real cornerstone of success in sales—getting out to see the customer. It's so simple, yet too many salespeople just don't get it.

For the record, the salesman was Edgar Rand, who went on to become chairman of the board for International Shoe. That's quite a story, and it can serve as an inspiration to anyone who wants to succeed in life. In other words, get out there and make things happen. That's what life is all about—making every day a productive and positive experience. If you are in sales, that means seeing your customers regularly.

I've been in sales most of my life, and there are days when I get a little down. When that happens, I've found that the greatest antidote is making a call on a customer. That's right, getting out there where the action is and making calls on real live customers, not sitting in the office doing paperwork or making phone calls. Sure, phone calls have to be made and reports have to be written, but all of those administrative tasks are secondary.

You can wear the latest in clothes, have a master's degree, and look terrific with your summer tan, but if you are in sales and don't want to inconvenience yourself by getting out in the field, you should consider getting out of the business. On the other hand, you may simply be an old farm boy who has the common sense to figure out what sales is all about.

48
Develop a healthy paranoia

INVARIABLY THE PHONE CALL goes something like this: "I can't believe it. I've been calling on that person for years, and I've done everything they've asked me to do, but they still went ahead and gave their business to our competitor. I'm really upset." We've all seen such scenarios played out one way or another. The words may be different, but what it amounts to is that an account has been lost.

The moment the salesman first hears the bad news, it's everyone's fault but his own. Price comes into play, but no matter how sweet the deal or how low the price, if you look into the circumstances of what happened, taking things for granted comes into play. I'm not saying this is always the case, but nine times out of ten it's the root of the problem.

It's part of human nature to take things for granted. That's because it's comfortable and less stressful to believe everything is OK. Why should any of us have to keep reinventing the wheel? Why should we have to go out of the way continually to reassure a customer or a loved one that they're always high on our priority list? But no matter how many sales seminars we attend or how many marriage counselors a couple sees, we all still have a tendency to take things for granted.

The fact is, nothing in life is guaranteed. Anyone in sales who doesn't understand that will face crisis after crisis and lose a lot of business and commissions. One has to learn how to develop what

I call a *healthy paranoia.* You have to stay on top of your accounts at all times and believe that your competitors will be coming to see your clients right after you leave. Really—that's the secret of all top salespeople. They take nothing for granted, including their employment.

The true sales professionals are always restless. They're constantly worrying about their accounts. That's tough, but selling is tough. People who like 9-to-5 jobs shouldn't be in sales. The pros are always coming up with new ideas for their clients. They send birthday cards to secretaries who help them get through to clients. They remember customers' birthdays and the names of their spouses and their children. They listen intently to what their customers have to say, whether it's personal or professional. They make sure customers know they care and care very much.

But we are all so busy these days that sometimes we let a birthday slip by or skip a chance to see an old customer because he said on the phone that everything was fine. Never fall into that trap.

Nothing can ever replace the personal visit. That's because you can look the person in the eye when you make your sales pitch. It's because you can take your customer to lunch or dinner or to a ball game to help cement the relationship. It also shows customers how sincere you are about providing good service. They know you're not taking their business for granted, because you are there—*in person.*

That's what sales is all about—not a voice mail message, not a fax, not a telephone call—a personal call. It's the best way to get business and keep business.

Something else I try to instill in my colleagues is the basic tenet never to assume anything. Don't assume you have the order until it's in your hand. Don't assume your job is secure just because you show up every day and work regular hours. There just might be someone else who will work longer hours and come up with new ways to do the job. Never assume the plane will leave on time or that your rental car is waiting for you. I don't want to turn everyone into a nervous wreck, but I'll bet most of us have been the victim of a canceled flight or a disappearing rental car reservation. Always check ahead. More important, check all of your appointments at least a day ahead of time so you know when you make your calls that your customers are expecting you.

What I'm trying to tell you is simple. Never assume. Always be on the alert for surprises. It pays to pay attention. Use common sense and practice good manners. Taking a customer for granted is the kiss of death, but it happens all the time.

Be there more often than your competitors. Be there when the customer needs you. If not, that customer may never need you again.

49
Making a call sends the blues running

 A GOOD FRIEND of mine—and a top salesperson— was feeling blue. She told me she didn't feel like doing anything that particular day because the business just didn't seem to be out there. I understood how she was feeling, and when she asked me for advice, I offered her what I believe is the best prescription for any salesperson in that state of mind—go out and make a call.

That's right, get out into the field and see your customers. Who knows, someone might even give you an order. Whenever I feel down or I find it hard to motivate myself, I've always found that getting out to see my customers is the greatest antidote. It's natural to get down once in a while. That's just the way life is. It's especially tough for salespeople. We have to be up so much of the time and on stage so often that it isn't possible always to be in top form. The trick is to find a way to get yourself on track again.

That's why I recommend calling on customers as the way to go. Customers are a salesperson's lifeblood. If you're doing a good job, they're what turn you on. Making things happen for your customers is what selling is all about. The tragedy is that too many salespeople don't understand this simple formula for success.

The sales call requires a couple of very basic things. First, you have to get out of the office. Most great sales are not made on the phone. They're made going one-on-one, in person, with a customer. Second, the salesperson must get organized and motivated for the call. You need to be fired up!

I'll tell you a story about one of the most successful salespeople I know. I wasn't there when the incident happened, but knowing the person and how he feels about selling, I'm sure it happened just the way it was related to me. The director of human resources for a large publishing company came into town to talk to all the salespeople in the Chicago branch office about the company's new pension plan. The meeting started at 9 o'clock on a Monday morning and was supposed to last about an hour. But the fellow making the presentation wasn't very good at it, and the meeting lasted much longer than anticipated. My friend became restless. Mondays are important for salespeople, and he wanted to get organized for the week. As the meeting dragged on, he finally told the director, "Sir, if you have this information in a brochure, I'll be glad to read it later, but right now I have better things to do than sit here wasting valuable selling time. Thank you." He then asked to be excused and went about his business.

You see, being out there with his customers was his No. 1 priority, and that's the way it should be. Pensions, profit-sharing plans, and other fringe benefits can only come about if salespeople are out in the field making their companies successful.

Top-performing salespeople make lots of calls. They don't waste time gossiping and drinking coffee. They're action-oriented people who love competition. They worry about their competitors and know as much about their competitors' products as they do about their own. They stay in touch with their clients, making sure they're getting the high level of service they deserve. They never take anything for granted, and that's why they're so successful.

I've read the latest books about the new breed of salespeople and how much smarter they are and how they fit into a team environment. You can talk all you want about new techniques and technologies, but some things will never change. The value of making personal calls is one of them.

So get off your duff and call on a customer. It'll do wonders for your attitude.

50

Enthusiasm now pays off in the future

 I'LL CALL THIS the "When's the next plane to Seattle?" story. It was told to me by the top health care sales honcho of a *Fortune* 500 company.

The conversation started with our reminiscing about some of the great salesmen both of us had known as well as the bosses who had trained us and helped form our values as salespeople. We had both been lucky, because we were taught by exceptional role models early in our careers. These teachers were committed individuals who believed in their companies and their products. They were true self-starters, characters who understood intuitively what the selling process was all about and who took great pride in being salesmen. But let me get back to the Seattle story.

The sales executive telling the story related how he had received word that a particular account he had worked on for months wasn't going to do business with his company even though he and his boss had felt they had landed the sale. The account was one of the major medical centers in Seattle and was worth millions in sales. The fellow telling me the story was then

129

simply an ordinary salesman doing everything he could to advance his career. He had good days and bad and worried about his future and how he could support his wife and two children, the kinds of things all of us think about.

After spending an incredible amount of time cultivating the key people at the medical center, the salesman got the word that he wasn't going to get the business, so it came time to tell his boss the bad news. That's never easy, and he was more than a little apprehensive. Anyway, he finally went in to see his boss and tell him what happened. As the story goes, as soon as he got the words out of his mouth, his boss asked: "When's the next plane to Seattle?" An hour later, the salesman and his boss were on their way to the airport.

They arrived in Seattle late that night, and early the next morning they were at the medical center asking to see the CEO. They tried all day, but it wasn't until 4:30 that afternoon that they got an audience with the top guy. The answer was still no even after they spent about forty-five minutes trying to change the decision. They were both crestfallen and returned to their West Coast regional offices. No, it wasn't a happy ending, but that really isn't the end of the story.

About six years later, the CEO they had flown up to see had relocated to another medical center, and the salesman had become a regional manager with his company. As chance would have it, he was attempting to sell the very same chief executive he and his old boss had struck out with years earlier. This time he was successful.

During the final meeting, the CEO made a statement that went something like this: "About six years ago when I was in Seattle, two men from this company made a call on me even though they both knew we had gone with one of their competitors. It was simply too late to change the decision at that time, but I have to tell you I was so impressed with their perseverance, their enthusiasm, and their commitment that I made a promise to myself that sometime in the future I wanted to do business with a company that had people who cared so much about what they had to sell."

Isn't that a great story? Doesn't that say so much? It says

never, ever give up. You never know how what you do today might lead to very positive results in the future. In other words, every call you make today, tomorrow, and next week is important. It might not pay off right away, but somewhere down the road—in some cases years later—it surely will.

How many of us are ready to take "the next plane to Seattle"? How many of us are that enthusiastic, and how many of us are that competitive? Don't sit there stewing. Do yourself a favor and get on that next plane to Seattle or Boston or Charlotte or wherever you have to go to get the business. That shows commitment and enthusiasm, and that impresses people, whether you make the sale or not. People remember those things, so don't be afraid to show that you care. Eventually it pays off.

51
Friendship and business do go together

RECENTLY A BUSINESS COLLEAGUE sent me an article on the subject of friendship that I found to be quite provocative. Some people think that friendship and business don't go together, but to my way of thinking this article proves just the opposite.

The article quoted Mark McCormack, whom I've referred to on pages 93 and 94. In this article, Mr. McCormack, author of *What They Don't Teach You at Harvard Business School* (Bantam, 1984) and its sequel, *What They Still Don't Teach You at Harvard Business School* (Bantam, 1990), is quoted as saying something that's crucial for people in sales to remember: "All things being equal, people will buy from a friend. All things being not quite so equal, people will still buy from a friend."

Please think about that. That's why it's so important to get close to your customers—to find out about their personal habits,

131

triumphs, and tragedies—in short, to pay attention to them. Make that phone call to wish a customer happy birthday or to ask, "Is your wife feeling better after her surgery?"

Cynics would probably say that you're using people when you behave that way and that you're showing concern because you expect some benefit in return. I don't buy that, because if you're serious about your business and you're dedicated to doing the best for your customers, then being concerned about them personally is natural. And it's natural for someone who's sincere.

Being a good friend in business shouldn't be confined to clients. It should also include your fellow workers. But whether it's business friends or colleagues, knowing how to get along with others is paramount in building relationships.

Robert B. Tucker, author of the article that quotes Mr. McCormack, shows how important this can be: "Many highly competent people never rise to their full potential in the business world because they can't get along with people." You and I see this phenomenon all the time, but it doesn't have to be that way.

Learn how to get along with others and see what you've been missing.

52
Look like a pro

 ONE OF MY PET PEEVES has to do with the way some people perceive their jobs. It also involves discipline and manners—two of my favorite subjects. To put it bluntly, a lot of individuals have become lazy not only in their work but in how they dress.

Consider this scenario: You're unemployed and have been searching for a job for months. You're getting frustrated by all the down time. You want to be back in the midst of the action. You're confident you could do a great job for any company that offers you the chance to prove yourself.

Then it happens. You get a phone call to come in for an interview. You know the company well. It's the best in the field, pays top dollar, and because of your background you would make a perfect fit. What a break! The company needs a salesperson in a certain territory immediately. Your appointment is Friday, first thing in the morning. You also know this company has casual days on Fridays. How are you going to dress for your interview?

You shouldn't even have to think about it. You dress professionally, of course, just as you would if you were making a sales call. You put your best foot forward to impress others. So why is it that more and more people, after they're hired, undergo a change in mind-set? Suddenly they want to go casual. Presenting a professional image no longer becomes a priority.

To me, being dressed properly for business is a must for anyone who wants to demonstrate professionalism. This is especially true of salespeople, who many years ago were thought of as glad-handers and were almost always considered to be on the shady side. Maybe a better description would be "snake oil" types. Let's just say salespeople didn't have a good reputation. But that image gradually began to change as companies woke up to the fact that salespeople who were properly trained and professionally dressed were taken more seriously by customers and potential clients. But it goes beyond that.

Casual attire is OK in its place. As with anything else, there is a time and a place to dress casually—a party, for instance, or a restaurant that doesn't have a formal dress code. For the record, nobody loves dressing in casual clothes more than I do. It's great fun and makes things so much more relaxed. But there are times when dressing more formally is a prerequisite. It conveys respect and shows a certain discipline that can be important to customers and colleagues.

I would never think of calling on one of my valued customers dressed casually. It's simply bad taste. It would show disrespect and make it appear that my company employs a bunch of yahoos. But then maybe some people don't really care. Maybe you think it

133

doesn't matter how a person dresses. You might believe that whether you wear a suit—or a polo shirt and a pair of chinos—is your prerogative. If that's the case, then get out of sales.

Think about it. When you're dealing with someone you're buying from, what do you look for? Usually, you look for someone who's clean and dresses appropriately. Casual dress can portray a lackadaisical attitude that borders on arrogance. I don't like giving my money to people who are casual about receiving it, and I expect someone who's selling me something to show me respect.

I know some of these things may sound old-fashioned, but I don't think they are. Good manners are always in vogue, and people with good manners always show respect for others. Now, I know some people will disagree with my premise. However, understand that part of being a professional entails dressing in a way that promotes a professional image.

Remember too that you represent more than just yourself. A lot of people are counting on you to keep the organization running. The sales staff is key to the success of any outfit. The way you behave and the way you present yourself is crucially important to everyone—customers and colleagues.

Many years ago, my first boss was a fellow by the name of Jim Dunn. He was the manager of the St. Louis office of *Life* magazine. A few years later he became the national advertising director, and after leaving Time Inc., he became publisher of *Forbes* magazine. As a former naval officer in World War II, he was a strict disciplinarian. He also was one heck of a salesman, who already had become a legend at *Life* magazine for his knack of cracking tough accounts.

One day when I arrived at work, he asked me to come into his office and proceeded to chew me out for my appearance. He put it this way: "Stetson is one of our accounts, and you don't even wear a hat. Go out and get one. Where is your tie clip? That tie is all over the place, and you look like a college boy. Shape up and dress properly. Look the part of a top salesman. People expect it of you. Be sharp and act smart. Now get out there and sell." I've never forgotten his advice, and I still think of Jim before I go out on calls.

Let me return to that question of casual days. A lot of offices have dress code holidays—days when you can come into the office dressed casually. Surprisingly, many salespeople choose to dress as casually as the support personnel. I guess that's OK, but I don't encourage it. I believe salespeople and executives should dress as though they might get called out at any moment by a customer or potential client to make a presentation. That's being professional, and that's being disciplined.

We've all heard stories about a salesperson being called by a prospect or current customer and told to come over right away. It's the nature of the business. Would you want to go over dressed in jeans, gym shoes, and a flannel shirt? What kind of impression would that leave with your client? Is that what you would call professional attire? Absolutely not.

One of the excuses for salespeople dressing casually on a certain day is that they're coming in to do paperwork. But that's taking a whole day out of quality selling time. Paperwork should be done in the evenings and during other off-duty hours, not during prime time. If you want to be taken seriously, and if you want to succeed, then look like a professional and enjoy it, whether it's winter or summer.

Dressing appropriately is simply the right thing to do. That's Selling 101.

Act and look like a pro.

Getting the customer's attention— and what to do once you have it

53

Wrigley's, hot dogs, and the value of advertising

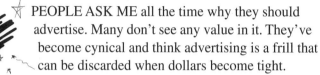 PEOPLE ASK ME all the time why they should advertise. Many don't see any value in it. They've become cynical and think advertising is a frill that can be discarded when dollars become tight. That's too bad, because advertising really works, and it's an economical way to keep in touch with customers.

One way I'd like to illustrate the point is by sharing a parable about the legendary William Wrigley, Jr. The man was a great believer in advertising and used the medium to tell the world how great his chewing gum was.

The story first ran as a promotional ad in our sister publication, *Advertising Age*. It's called "The Man Who Sold Chewing Gum," and it goes like this:

It was common knowledge among his colleagues that William Wrigley, Jr. attributed the success of his chewing gum empire to constant and forceful advertising.

Once he was traveling to California on the famous Super Chief with a young accountant from his firm. As they were reviewing the figures for the quarterly statement, the young man said, "Sir, Wrigley's gum is known and sold all over the world. We have a larger share of the market than all of our competitors combined. Why don't you save the millions you are spending on advertising and shift those dollars into the profit column for the next quarter?"

Wrigley thought for a moment and then asked, "Young man, how fast is this train going?"

"About sixty miles an hour," replied the young accountant.

>And Wrigley asked, "Then why doesn't the railroad remove
>the engine and let the train travel on its own momentum?"

That story has been around for a long time, and the message is as true today as ever. But it doesn't give the whole picture.

Let me put a little different twist on the subject with another promotional parable that used to run in *Advertising Age*. It's titled "The Hot Dog Man and the Recession." Here's the story:

>There once was a man who lived by the side of the road and sold hot dogs. In fact, he sold very good hot dogs.
>
>He put up highway signs telling people how good his hot dogs tasted. He stood by the side of the road and called out, "Buy a hot dog, mister?"
>
>And people bought his hot dogs. They bought so many hot dogs the man increased his meat and bun orders. He bought a bigger stove so he could meet his customers' demands. And finally, he brought his son home from college to help out in the family business.
>
>But something happened. His son said, "Father, don't you watch television or read the newspapers? Don't you know we're heading for a recession...[and that] the European situation is unstable and the domestic economy is getting worse?"
>
>And the father thought, "My son's a smart boy. He's been to college. He ought to know what he's talking about."
>
>So the man cut down his meat and bun orders, took down his highway signs, and no longer stood by the side of the road to sell his hot dogs.
>
>His sales fell almost overnight. "You're right, son," said the father. "We certainly are in a serious recession."

These are simple stories, but both have crucially important messages. I know companies today that have been wonderfully successful over the years by simply turning out quality products and promoting them with an aggressive and competent sales organization. They've backed up their sales forces with advertising, and the formula has worked well. But now they're holding

138

back on advertising because they can save a few bucks by doing so. The few thousand dollars they save might make the accountants happy, but they're likely to end up losing potential customers and market share because they strayed from their game plan. William Wrigley, Jr. understood this, as have his successors. "The Hot Dog Man and the Recession" tells a different story, warning of self-fulfilling prophecies.

The moral is that we must not listen to the doom-and-gloomers when they tell us how scary things are out there. Do what you do best, keep in touch with your customers, and the rest will take care of itself.

54
Advertising helps you tell your side

I'VE NEVER FORGOTTEN the story because I was there when it happened. It involves advertising and its role in business. Back when it occurred, most of the people I knew not only believed in advertising but understood how it worked.

At the time, which was quite a few years ago, I was the national sales director for one of the leading association medical journals in this country. The publication carried loads of pharmaceutical advertising. One company in particular would run three or four expensive, full-color ads in each weekly issue. But trouble—little did I know—lurked around the corner. The association that published the journal had a committee of pharmacologists who were soon to publish a guide to prescription drugs advising physicians about which medications work best for patients with certain conditions.

When the compendium was released I received one of the first copies, and, much to my horror, this advertiser's products didn't receive good reviews. The ad director of that company was hard-nosed and had a reputation for having a short temper. But I knew I had to call him first before he heard the bad news from someone else.

I told him what had occurred and what the compendium said about his company's products. Then I just held my breath waiting for his reaction. I was sure he would cancel all his advertising as a punitive measure against the association's journal. When he asked me how many advertising pages his company was running in each issue, I expected the worst. But I was wrong.

He then told me that he planned to double the number of pages in each issue because he believed the committee had erred in its assessment of his company's products. And he said there was no better way to correct that impression than by informing practicing physicians through ads that "accurately" explained the benefits of his company's medications.

Many years later that advertising manager became chairman of the company, and the company has become a worldwide pharmaceutical giant. The former manager has since retired, but I've never forgotten the wisdom he passed on to me about advertising. He told me that a page of advertising was the one thing a company could control in any magazine or journal to tell its side of the story on a regular basis. He also told me that counting on any publication to give a company favorable and consistent editorial mention just wasn't realistic.

That has stuck with me all these years because it makes so much sense. I think too many people in the advertising business today try to blend advertising with editorial, when one has nothing to do with the other. Advertising in any publication is a guest in the house, even if it does pay the bills. If used properly, it's a powerful marketing tool.

Sure, advertising can be expensive, but expecting editors to run puff pieces about a company simply because it's a big advertiser is expecting something that no first-rate magazine would do. That would be unethical and foolish because readers expect impartial and above-board coverage of the news in their area of interest. If they think favoritism or bias is being shown, they bail out fast.

Consequently, if you believe that a publication truly reaches the audience you want to sell, certainly do everything you can to educate that publication's editors about your company. Most editors are quite willing to listen to any organization that seeks an audience with them and brings news and information that would be useful to their readers.

On the other hand, don't expect favorable treatment just because you're an advertiser. That isn't what gets the job done. What does? A lot of things, most of all whether whatever you're doing or selling is of interest to the audience.

Lauer at length: Distinguish yourself by mastering the art of public speaking

PUBLIC SPEAKING CAN BE FUN, or at least that's what the books offering advice on the subject say. But it takes preparation, flexibility, humility, and a sense of humor.

Talking in front of people and having them take stock of you has to be one of the most difficult things a person can be called to do. But once you learn how to give a first-class presentation, public speaking can offer you all sorts of opportunities to communicate to different groups and even to become a spokesperson for your company or a particular industry. If you can master the basics of public speaking, you'll be a leg up on everyone else. In a sense, it makes you stand out from your colleagues and peers.

As with anything else, the more you practice public speaking, the better you become. But don't go into it with any illusions, because it's filled with booby traps.

I'm invited frequently to give talks to various groups across the country. I've spoken at sales meetings, hospital board retreats, vendor executive committee meetings, and a variety of other gatherings. The locations have ranged from plush and exotic vacation spas to small meeting rooms in a variety of hotels and motels, some nice and some not so nice.

Despite all this experience, before I speak I'm always nervous as all get out. There's a churning in my stomach, my palms turn sweaty, and sometimes I just about come unglued. But that's all part of the experience. It's how I used to feel before a football game or hockey game, and most certainly before I took a final exam. But that's usually when you do your best. Being fired up about something means your adrenaline is flowing.

Over the years I've experienced some things and learned some lessons about public speaking that may help you avoid some of the pitfalls I've encountered.

What are some tricks of the trade?

First, there's a cardinal rule: Never, but *never*, drink before you speak. Things are tough enough without mixing booze into the equation.

Luncheon and after-dinner speakers often are tempted to have a drink before speaking. There you are at some beautiful resort with a bunch of vibrant and upbeat sales types, and wouldn't it be fun to have a vodka and tonic or a cold beer to relax a little before your talk or presentation. I have seen individuals who have tried to "relax" by gulping down a couple of drinks, usually with embarrassing results. Don't even think about it.

If you do have a drink, it takes the edge off things and saps both your energy and your enthusiasm. Remember, a lot of people are expectantly waiting to hear what you have to say. If you've taken a drink of alcohol, you've not only let your audience down, you've let yourself down.

You should begin your preparation by drawing up an outline of what you want to say. This is absolutely essential if you are to have any success at all. I've seen some very accomplished speakers fall flat on their faces because they didn't do their homework. They tried to "wing it," which just doesn't work, even for most pros. Before you do anything else, get organized. That's really the secret of success in anything—being prepared.

I always speak from prepared notes or sometimes even a full

text. Simply getting up and rambling on for thirty to forty-five minutes usually doesn't work. Sure, some individuals can do it, but they're usually professionals who give speeches for a living. If you really want to score points with your audience, they appreciate speakers who've done their homework and are prepared. It shows respect, and any audience likes to feel that the speaker respects their intelligence. It's just good manners.

Next, consider how many people you will be speaking to. Is it ten? fifty? one hundred? The size of the audience is vital, because if you're planning to use visual aids to make your points, you need to tailor them so everyone can see them properly. How many times have all of us sat through presentations where the speaker is trying to make points while using slides no one can read? When that happens, it detracts from the message. You get the impression the speaker either didn't prepare or tried to do things on the cheap.

Always arrive at least an hour before you're scheduled to speak, to gain some measure of composure and also to check out the location where you'll be speaking. You also should check to see whether the meeting is running on time. Some meetings get way off schedule, and in rare instances you may even be asked to speak earlier than planned. This is also the time to check on a couple of other basics. If you're the luncheon or after-dinner speaker, make sure the microphone and podium are set up. Recently I was scheduled to speak to a group of three hundred people at a fine hotel in Charleston, South Carolina. When I checked to see if there was a microphone and a podium in the room, I found that the person in charge had forgotten to get both.

Then there's the length of the presentation. Here's the tough part. Don't take too long to make your points. Remember that your listeners have time constraints just as you do. You may be the most riveting speaker, and you may have the funniest stories, but if you take too long, you'll lose your audience.

Then there's the whole subject of jokes. It can be fun to start off a talk with a little story or a joke. Humor at the beginning of a talk can bring the audience over to your side almost immediately. It's a tactic experienced speakers use all the time.

Humor helps in any presentation, but make sure that it's

144

appropriate. Be careful. What's funny to you isn't necessarily funny to other people. You might offend someone right at the beginning of your talk. Off-color stories are out of bounds, no matter what. Frankly, I try to stay away from all jokes. They're a nice way to loosen up your audience, but if you've got a good message to communicate, that's what everyone came to hear, not your imitation of Bob Hope, Bob Newhart, or Henny Youngman.

And, of course, always speak with enthusiasm and energy. Audiences love to listen to individuals who not only know what they're talking about but who also do it with conviction. There's nothing worse than listening to someone delivering a speech in a monotone, lackluster manner—no matter how much they know about the subject. Make every talk you give a special event, and also make sure your audience knows from the moment you begin talking that you feel very privileged to be with them. They'll recognize your feelings right away.

But there's something even more important than all these things I have touched on. That's learning by observing other speakers and presenters. Watch how they do it, and try to copy their strong points. Go out of your way to talk to them about how they prepare for a speech or presentation. Most will be happy to give you some valuable pointers.

Also read everything you can about public speaking. There are plenty of good how-to books out there. Follow the advice of the authors and then practice what they preach. Practice at home with your family and practice at the office with colleagues you respect and trust.

Probably the most effective tool there is for learning how to give a presentation is videotaping yourself. That's really the best teacher. It shows you just the way you appear to others, spotlighting both your strengths and your weaknesses. Yes, it can be pretty devastating, but it works.

So there you have it, a few observations from someone who gives talks and presentations more frequently than most. But everything I've told you won't mean a thing unless you're willing to work hard at becoming a more skillful speaker. The art of public speaking can be a boon to anyone's career—and a lot of

145

fun—but it takes common sense, discipline, and, above all, practice. Who knows, if you work really hard at it, you may become a spokesperson for your industry. I can assure you that there will be a premium placed on that special talent now and in the years ahead.

Most people don't want to put in the effort to do all the things necessary to give a first-class presentation, and that's why you can distinguish yourself from your colleagues and competitors if you learn to do so.

Go for it!

56
When the real selling starts

 RECENTLY A NUMBER of my colleagues and I were sitting around talking about selling. These individuals were all solid salespeople with outstanding track records, but they expressed dissatisfaction with how difficult it was to get in to see certain people. And people who don't return phone calls seemed to be a particular annoyance. My colleagues just couldn't fathom why some people behave that way and wondered what I thought about this particular phenomenon. I told them that unreturned phone calls are just part of the business of selling. The trick is to get through to those hard-to-reach individuals by some-how getting their attention.

My message was clear: Selling is not an easy game. It's filled with heavy doses of rejection and meeting all kinds of people who don't want to see you or hear what you have to say. For some reason, too many people in sales today seem to think that the customers should come to them. I guess it's OK to feel that way, but in the real world, selling takes persistence and perseverance.

146

Anybody who's ever succeeded in this business learns never to give up on getting through to the people who make the buying decisions. That's the reason any business hires a sales force. If it were as easy as making a phone call and getting through right away, a few telemarketers would do just fine, and companies could do away with an awful lot of expense.

Selling is one of the most demanding professions there is. Notice I use the word *profession.* That's because it takes a special type of person and a certain set of skills to be successful at this discipline. It looks so easy to people on the outside, but any one of us in the business knows how difficult it can be. We know, because we've all been through periods of disappointment. That goes with the territory. The best stories in sales are about those who endure and somehow get the "impossible" appointments and then land the accounts.

Many years ago I was the Midwest manager for a major trade publishing company. I had only been with the company for a few months, so I wasn't too well versed in the gossip and taboos of the Chicago office. But suddenly a special advertising space became available in one of the magazines that I represented, and I remembered seeing an ad in another magazine that was perfect for our available spot. So, being young and filled with enthusiasm, I called the top ad person at the company that had run the advertisement and asked to speak with him. I told the man's secretary what I was trying to do, and she promised to give her boss my message. When he didn't telephone, I made four more phone calls over the next few days and in each case apologized to the secretary for my persistence.

Then one evening, about 5:30, I was sitting at my desk writing some letters when my phone rang. It was the man I had been trying to reach for several days. After I made my proposal, he said he would get back to me. Sure enough, the next morning he gave me the order.

When I called my boss in New York to tell him the good news, he wouldn't believe me. His words went something like this: "That guy won't talk to anybody from our company. We fired a good friend of his a couple of years ago, and he hasn't seen any of

147

our reps since." When the order came in, he finally believed me. But if I had listened to all the doom-and-gloom stories, I'm not sure I would have made the initial contact.

There are actually two points here: Don't listen to the supposed shibboleths about certain accounts, and don't take unreturned phone calls as a personal affront. They're routine in sales. Rejection happens no matter what business you're in, but it's especially true in sales. Just remember—never give up.

As a matter of fact, many top salespeople don't feel challenged until someone tells them no. That's when the real selling starts.

57

Determination and persistence yield rich rewards

 DETERMINATION AND PERSISTENCE are two characteristics that any salesperson is going to need in an increasingly competitive environment in order to succeed. I can't tell you how many meetings I've sat through where, invariably, the question is asked: "How do we get to the people at the top who make the decisions?" There's really no simple answer to this question except that dogged determination can make a difference. Let me explain.

You may have read about this before, but it's one of my favorite sales stories, and I enjoy telling it. Some time ago I was invited to address a group of architectural designers on the topic of health care reform. The meeting was in Chicago at the world-famous Merchandise Mart. There were about fifteen people present, and they all seemed interested in what I saw down the road for the health care industry.

After my monologue, there was a question-and-answer period followed by a discussion of how difficult it was to get in to see a CEO. By this time, everyone had arrived at the same conclusion: The CEO is the one who needs to be sold on any kind of major project or expenditure. That person is the ultimate decision maker. Without his or her approval, no project can get off the ground.

The discussion went on for quite a while. Sitting across from me was a young lady who stayed quiet throughout the give and take. Finally, as the moderator, I asked her how she felt about the difficulty in gaining access to CEOs. The young lady, who represented a well-known carpet manufacturer, gave an answer that was to the point. It went something like this: "I am really proud of my management. All along, they have taught me to go to the top to sell our carpeting. This year I sold more carpeting to health care facilities than anyone else in the country. The way it has worked for me is that I start calling CEOs at 6 A.M. You would be surprised how many times I actually reach them at that time in the morning. If I don't reach them then, I start calling after 6 P.M. I also get through to a lot of them at that time. It's that simple, and I've been very lucky."

That's her story, and it's a classic. She used plain old common sense to get to the person who makes the decisions. As she realized, most CEOs get into the office early and stay late. There's no wizardry in her technique, just determination and persistence. She chose not to listen to the doom-and-gloomers who told her it was impossible to reach the person at the top.

Ingenuity is involved too. This young woman had the courage to try something a lot of others wouldn't. Her payoff? She sold millions of yards of carpeting and made a lot of money. Of course, in order to do so, she had to get up extra early and stay late, but that all goes along with being a winner.

The rewards of winning will belong to those who step out smartly and aggressively. The rewards will belong to those who want to compete, not sit on the sidelines, and to those who employ

149

courage and determination. And the rewards will belong to those who ask for the order.

So get out there and have the best year you've ever had. Opportunity is everywhere.

58
Come quickly to the point

 AT FIRST I THOUGHT it was something I alone was dealing with, but as I've talked to others I've begun to realize many people are trying to cope with the same problem. It's kind of a tough one to handle, because most of us don't like hurting other people's feelings. Then again there are only so many hours in the day, and we all have a job to do. I'm referring to people who get you on the phone and then go on and on about this and that without ever getting to the point. Don't get me wrong. I love schmoozing, but there's a time and a place for it, and that's *not* when we're under time constraints.

The same principle applies to individuals who ask you to join them in a meeting, and, once they have you seated, talk about everything but the very matter the meeting was supposed to address. It wastes time and is just plain rude. The cardinal rule of dealing with others should be: *Never overstay your welcome.*

As a salesman, I was taught to get on and off the phone without any fanfare and to be cognizant of others' time. Today when I take calls from salespeople, many seem intent on getting everything they can into the first contact. That kind of selling turns me off.

The real tragedy of what I'm talking about is when someone you've known for years never seems to learn proper phone etiquette for business. The telephone isn't an instrument designed to waste time and money, although in the wrong hands it frequently does just that. Rather, it's a communications tool that, when used effectively and professionally, can help a person accomplish great things, including making a lot of money.

Now voice mail has been added to the communications maze. Frankly, I'm convinced that voice mail is another time waster. If you don't believe me, call one of the airlines and listen to all the instructions you're given for how to use the system that is supposedly designed to expedite your call. Think about it. You, the customer, are treated like a five-year-old, when you should be treated like the most important individual the airline will do business with that day. You're made to feel like a number—just another person lost in the crowd.

It's bad business, and it's bad communications, because these machines can't think, and they have no feelings. Sometimes, employing such technology in the name of saving money is like stepping over dollars to get to pennies.

Getting back to the subject of meetings, I'm opposed to most of them because they, too, usually go on much too long without really accomplishing anything. If you want to have a meeting, go ahead and have one, but don't waste anyone's time. State the purpose of the gathering, discuss what you promised you'd discuss, and then let everyone get back to work. People will love you for it, because short meetings have really become something of an oddity these days.

The same thing can be said about memos. They also must be quick to make the point. They shouldn't be instruments to show others how smart you are, and they shouldn't be ponderous epistles that bore the recipients. In other words, make them short and sweet.

Brevity is the spice of life. In all you do, be direct but not rude. Respect others' precious time, and in doing so you will become an effective communicator. Long-winded chats about the weather or last night's ball game are fine in a social setting, but at work, remember that everyone's time is at a premium.

59

'Tis better to listen than to schmooze

ONE OF THE GREATEST attributes anyone in sales can have is the ability to listen. Many years ago, listening wasn't even in the sales lexicon. The stereotype of a salesperson was someone who liked to drink, could tell a lot of good stories, and always wore a big smile. Unfortunately, at some companies that stereotype is alive and well. Salespeople often are seen as gregarious buffoons who know how to have a good time and turn in big expense accounts. But times have changed, and so have the people in sales.

The techniques of selling have also changed markedly. It's far more important today to be a good listener than a good schmoozer. Salespeople must listen to customers, colleagues, supervisors, and anyone else who can help make a sale. Selling is so complicated today that sales professionals need all the help they can get.

Good salespeople are sponges for information. They read and absorb all the information they can lay their hands on. They also seek out the senior sales staff at their organizations to learn how they do their jobs. They listen to the stories they tell about how they got in to see the key person or what they had to do to land that big account. This entails a certain amount of humility and quite a bit of time, but the things you can learn from these sessions are invaluable. They're also lessons you won't find in any training manual.

While learning from your colleagues is a good place to start, the most important part of selling is the ability to listen to your customers. Actually, it can be broken down into listening with your eyes, ears, and head. Listening is much more than simply sitting still as someone drones on about this and that. It's the ability to do a variety of things in order to really understand a customer.

Some years ago, Julius Fast wrote a book titled *Body Language* (Pocket Books, 1988). I keep it around to remind me about some of the basic elements of quality listening. In the book, Mr. Fast says that when you're with customers, you can get some indication of how they feel about what you're saying by the way they're sitting. For instance, if their arms are folded across their chests, they're probably signaling that they're resistant to your message. There are other telltale signs, but the point is that anyone with a skilled eye can get a pretty good picture of what's going on in a customer's head.

Of course there's also the message you can hear. Most customers will give a salesperson all the ammunition needed to make the sale. But too often the salesperson is so intent on making the sale that he or she isn't alert to what the customer is trying to say. I was with one salesperson who already had been given an order by the customer but went right ahead and made the pitch even though the customer was strapped for time. That shows a lack of listening—and a lack of common courtesy.

Then there's listening with your head. Sometimes it's what customers don't tell you that's more important than what they say. That's where experience and a sixth sense come into play. You have to know your customers well in order to practice this technique, which is why personal calls are so important.

Remember that listening is more important today than ever before, and any salesperson who wants to become more skillful should learn all the facets of effective listening. It's basic stuff, but remember that good listeners know when to speak and when to remain silent. It just takes practice.

60
Keep your goal in focus

LACK OF FOCUS in an organization can manifest itself in at least two ways. A common one is a preoccupation with all the bells and whistles that go along with success: state-of-the-art computers, E-mail, office suites, and everything else that comes into play in a corporate setting. All these things can be important tools for any smooth-running company, but they shouldn't detract from the basic business. There's only one preoccupation that should be paramount—the needs of the customer.

In the face of the electronic sophistication we have today, I am dead-set against any sales organization greeting potential customers with an automated telephone answering system. It's just not the way it should be done. People like to be treated with dignity and respect. The least we can do is greet customers personally.

In the name of efficiency, too many businesses have forgotten how to take care of a customer the right way. That means with care, nurturing, and personal attention. Expressions such as "May I help you?" or "Thank you for calling," spoken by an honest-to-goodness live person, are invaluable for giving communication that personal touch. Such gestures make all the difference in the world, because they give the impression a company cares. It's the only way to go. At least that's what I was taught, and that's what I believe.

A second way organizations lose focus is by failing to keep things simple. Day-to-day business is tough enough, but companies like to complicate things with all sorts of add-ons. In some circles they're called *promising profit centers*. These are usually acquired on the flimsy premise that they will somehow give employees new vistas to conquer. But then look at what happens.

Companies are going through the ordeal of having to lop off businesses they added a few years ago when things were going well. Now when the bottom line doesn't look too promising, the executives of those companies are downsizing to their core businesses.

Stay with what you do best and make it run even better.

61
Add a touch of intimacy: Write personal notes

 THERE'S SOMETHING ABOUT A NOTE addressed to you in someone's own handwriting that commands immediate attention. I think it's because somebody has taken the time to sit down and actually write you a message. There's an intimacy you don't get from a typewritten letter or an E-mail. If you really want to get someone's attention, jot a note in your own hand. I can virtually guarantee you it will be read. It always works with me.

But how many of us take the time to do that? Probably not many. Writing takes additional effort and thought, whereas there could be a form letter that's already typed up that would fill the bill. Or I'll often hear people say they just don't have the time to write a personal note. There just aren't enough hours in the day. Those are common excuses, but I think it goes deeper than that. I think a lot of people are either embarrassed about their ability to write in longhand or worry that putting something on paper in their own handwriting might reveal too much of themselves. I say that's silly, and that's especially true if you're in sales.

Selling involves intimacy. There's a chemistry between a

155

salesperson and a customer that's hard to describe, but it's there. That's why video hookups or an exchange of faxes will never replace the personal call and the handshake. A lot of companies are experimenting with new techniques for selling because they want to save money. They think they've really stumbled onto something significant. But it won't work. Don't ever under-estimate the personal call. And never underestimate the needs of your customers. To salespeople, they're everything.

Sending a handwritten note to thank a customer for a sale or wishing him or her a happy anniversary adds a nice touch of intimacy. It's the kind of thing really professional, successful salespeople do all the time. They go out of their way to cement their relationships with clients.

But there are other ways to stay in touch with a client or prospect. There's the quick telephone call to say thank you for a piece of business or to ask if there are any problems. Too many salespeople worry about the next sale and forget about current customers.

Keeping customers is as important as getting new ones. Too frequently, established customers are taken for granted. One way to make sure this isn't happening is to call or stop by from time to time to make sure all is well. Many of the top salespeople I know also make sure their clients get a card on their birthdays and other special occasions. Taking an interest in a client's family life conveys intimacy and commitment. Now, I'm not talking about phoniness or feigning interest when you really don't give a hoot. That type of behavior only backfires. If you have a problem with being sincere, you probably shouldn't be in sales in the first place.

I'm talking about simple things: a note, a phone call, interest in a customer's personal life. The point is, you shouldn't be afraid to let your clients know how much you care and appreciate them. They make your life richer in so many ways.

62

A master teaches
good manners and common sense

I STILL HEAR STORIES about the late Karl Bays, probably the greatest salesman the health care industry ever knew. This was the man who took American Hospital Supply Co. to new heights before it was taken over by Baxter International in one of the most compelling and controversial buyouts the health care industry has ever seen. He became chairman of Baxter before leaving it to head up IC Industries, now known as Whitman Industries. The man lives on in the hearts of everyone who knew him.

The story I heard about Karl came from Don Arnwine, the former head of Voluntary Hospitals of America, who now heads Arnwine & Associates, a management consulting firm in Dallas. I was dining with Don and his wife, Norma, in Dallas, and we were reminiscing about a lot of things, when Karl's name surfaced. Don talked about Karl's way with people and how much Don had respected him as a person and a friend.

Anyway, as the story goes, Karl and Don were sitting around a table somewhere in Dallas, a few years earlier, when the topic of sales came up. Karl Bays made this observation: "Selling is made up of two components. One is common sense and the other is good manners." Think about that for a moment. To my way of thinking, he captured the very essence of selling.

Good manners and common sense. You really can't have one without the other, simply because anybody with common sense will invariably practice good manners when dealing with clients and prospects.

Let me repeat it: good manners. It's all very basic, and it's

157

easy: saying thank you and please; addressing people as sir or ma'am; standing up when someone comes into an office to greet you; being on time for appointments; being prepared for calls; waiting for your clients to be seated before you sit down, either in an office setting or when entertaining them for lunch or dinner; and being careful not to offend anyone with profanity or with an off-color story.

Most of us in sales practice good manners every day, but, believe me, I run into salespeople who violate all the rules all the time. Either they don't know what good manners are or they haven't been trained properly. It doesn't matter which is the case. Such people just aren't going to make it in this business. Good manners separate the professionals from the amateurs. They're the icing on the cake and can make all the difference in the world.

Good manners, the essence of a civilized society, are usually forgotten by the incompetents and losers. Everyone else is at fault, not them. You'll hear them say things like, "That's not my responsibility," or "That's not what I'm paid to do." Then there's "I couldn't make the sale, because they didn't like me." You know what I'm saying. They're part of the I-feel-sorry-for-myself crowd.

What about common sense? I'm talking about things such as getting out of someone's way when you see they're preoccupied with other matters. Give the customer a break and come back some other time. If you go on with your pitch, the customer isn't going to pay much attention to you anyway. Common sense has to do with making an appointment with your client or prospect, not just dropping in unexpectedly. Common sense has to do with being a person of integrity and reliability. Keep your word; carry through on your promises.

Common sense has to do with carrying business cards with you wherever you go and always having a pen in your pocket so you can jot down names or write out an order. Finally, common sense has to do with having the brains to ask for an order. After all, that's what the job is all about—making a sale so you can make money. Be proud of that.

Remember the words of Karl Bays. Good manners and common sense are traits always exhibited by the top producers. Observe, and you will see for yourself.

63

Body language can show you mean business—or don't

SOMETIMES A HEADLINE can really catch your eye. One that piqued my interest a while back was "Don't cross your legs"—along with the accompanying story that explained why that is good advice. The article appeared in *The Competitive Advantage*, a newsletter for sales and marketing professionals published out of Portland, Oregon.

The story discusses a study conducted by Gerard L. Nierenberg and Henry H. Calero, who videotaped two thousand sales transactions, looking for success secrets. They found that no sales were made by people who had their legs crossed. Nierenberg and Calero, by the way, are authors of *How to Read a Person Like a Book* (Pocket Books, 1982), and the results of their sales study are covered in the book.

For anyone in sales, actions such as crossing your legs, putting your hands on your face while you talk, and lack of eye contact are all fundamental don'ts, but sometimes we forget what we've been taught.

Take two salespeople. One works long, hard hours but with little success. The other works equally hard, but everything this person touches seems to turn to gold. Sure, luck plays a part, but after the variables are weeded out, other basics come into play.

159

Consider those crossed legs. Sitting in a customer's office with legs crossed sends out casual, relaxed vibes. But a salesperson who keeps both feet firmly planted on the floor and sits on the edge of the seat shows that this is someone who means business.

Then there's eye contact. Looking the other person in the eye should come naturally—not staring, simply giving the other person your undivided attention. That contact shows courtesy and respect and is part of good manners. Yet I've had salespeople call on me who will look everywhere but at me. It gives me the impression that they aren't focused and really aren't that interested in me. The customer should have your attention all the way through the visit, not just now and then. Furthermore, eye contact is a very discreet way to take control of a situation. Individuals who know how to influence others have terrific eye-contact skills. They have a knack for giving the impression a customer is the most important person in their lives.

Next: your hands. Keep them off your face. I've seen salespeople who talk to a customer or prospect with their hands literally over their mouths. It's very distracting, and the sales pitch often becomes unintelligible. Selling is next to impossible when the customer can't understand a word you're saying. Your hands should be either on your lap or turning the pages of a sales aid for the customer.

Effective body language conveys respect for the person you're talking to. Too many salespeople have ruined their careers by not being considerate and polite—with customers as well as colleagues. Treating others with dignity and respect will never go out of style.

64
Ravioli in slow motion, or,
What to order at a business lunch

THE BUSINESS LUNCH is an integral part of selling. But having lunch with a client or prospect can involve all kinds of booby traps. You could be committing a faux pas without realizing it. That's one of the key points made in an article I read in Northwest Airlines' *World Traveler* magazine. It was filled with much sage advice from experts on the art of business lunches.

According to Dee Soder, president of Endymion Executive Assessments and Advisory Services, based in New York, lunch actually might not be the appropriate time to discuss serious matters, because there are often too many distractions. Soder warns: "Right at the time of your pitch, the waiter or waitress might show up, or you might spill coffee." There's also the specter of offending the person you are dining with by eating or drinking the wrong thing. For instance, if your lunch partner is a vegetarian, he or she may not like you eating a piece of meat. Or the person may not approve if you order an alcoholic drink.

But what really caught my attention were some comments in the article by Marilyn Moats Kennedy, who was identified as president of Kennedy's Career Strategies in Chicago. Her remarks about what to order during a business lunch brought back some memories. She strongly recommends ordering something "you can eat gracefully." That precludes spaghetti or other precarious dishes. And I speak from personal experience.

There is one client lunch I will remember for the rest of my life. Some twenty years ago, when my employer, Crain

161

Communications, bought *Modern Healthcare* from McGraw-Hill, things were not so rosy. Business wasn't good, and many advertisers weren't happy with the uncertainty of a new owner. As the new publisher, I had to get into the field and settle things down. One of the first accounts I saw was Eastman Kodak Co. in Rochester, New York. The company was threatening to pull its advertising because of the poor reproduction of its ads.

Naturally, I asked the salesperson assigned to the account to join me on my visit to Rochester. The gentleman we called on seemed like a nice enough fellow, but we could tell by his body language that he was somewhat skeptical. The meeting lasted an hour, and then it was lunchtime. No resolution had been reached, and I was apprehensive about losing the prestigious account. So off we went to a nearby Italian restaurant.

We each had a beverage of some sort and ordered our food. After some more conversation, the food finally arrived. Little did I know that I was about to experience one of the most frightening episodes in my sales career.

My colleague had ordered ravioli that was swimming in Italian sauce. I ordered a sandwich, and our client had a salad. It didn't take long for disaster to strike. I saw it unfolding, almost in slow motion. As I watched my colleague raise his spoon to his mouth, I noticed that the ravioli wasn't centered properly in the spoon. It slid off and plopped back into the dish, splashing sauce all over our client. His suit, tie, shirt, and even his hair were splattered. I stopped breathing, my colleague turned bright red, and our client sat in stunned silence. As soon as I recovered, I leaped to my feet with napkin in hand in an attempt to repair the damage. Thoughts of never again seeing another Kodak ad grace the pages of *Modern Healthcare* raced through my head.

Then something magical happened. Our client started to chuckle at the absurdity of the situation. His chuckles soon turned into full-scale laughter, and we both joined in. From that day forward, the man would retell the story—with great guffaws— about that lunch and what befell him. And Eastman Kodak has been one of our major advertisers ever since. We were lucky indeed.

What's the point? Two, really. When you take a client to lunch, make sure you don't order anything that can splash. Second, make sure the customer you invite has a good sense of humor. Just in case.

By the way, soups are dangerous too.

65
Let competitors destroy themselves

YOU MIGHT HAVE HEARD the hubbub about a book titled *All's Fair: Love, War, and Running for President* (Simon & Schuster, 1994), co-authored by the married couple Mary Matalin and James Carville. In case those names don't sound familiar, Ms. Matalin was a key player in President Bush's 1992 campaign for re-election, and James Carville was the political strategist for Bill Clinton. Both are highly regarded in political circles, so their book makes for interesting reading if you're into political strategy and intrigue.

One statement that caught my eye as I perused the book was uttered by the late Republican strategist Lee Atwater. It pertains to all of us, especially those in sales: "Never interfere with your enemy while he's in the process of destroying himself." It makes a lot of sense, but it's a tough philosophy to live by if you're the competitive type, as most people in sales are.

It's hard when we find out that one of our competitors is attacking our products and maybe even making the attacks personal. But it goes on all the time. What should you do in response? As difficult as it might be, the best course of action is to do nothing. That's right, nothing.

Remember, if you've been doing your job properly and staying on top of your customer base, your clients know all about your products and probably have a pretty good handle on the kind of person you are. People who come in talking about their competition in a negative way and then making personal attacks are only hurting their own credibility. That kind of behavior invariably backfires. Don't lower yourself to that level.

Some things never go out of style no matter how fast the world seems to turn. I'm talking about ethics, morality, loyalty, and hard work. When you come right down to it, your reputation is something you alone can control, and how you choose to conduct yourself personally and professionally is going to stay with you. Sure, there are others who think otherwise. They have all the angles and because of their cynicism they are willing to cut corners and even lie to make a sale. In the short term it sometimes pays off, but in the long term it usually results in loss of business and loss of respect.

Customers like to do business with companies that believe in honesty and integrity. That's as true today as it was years ago. In the current competitive marketplace, there's no room for name-calling and unprofessional behavior. Those companies that concentrate their efforts on product development and fulfilling the needs of their customers are the ones that will win.

If there are competitors out there who do nothing but attack you and your company, they're committing suicide. They're giving you a boost every time they talk about you, and that's my point. Be grateful your competitor is that stupid, because it only plays into your hands. You can win by being a class act.

Most customers find it distasteful when anyone in the sales profession goes out of his or her way to attack another company. I don't like it, and I'm sure you don't either.

So, it looks like the late Mr. Atwater was right on target when he talked about never interfering when competitors are destroying themselves. Why bother? It's a waste of your valuable time. Just go make another call. That's the way to really beat your enemy. They forget what sales is all about—winning, not badmouthing the competition.

66
Money neurosis and closing the sale

MANY YEARS AGO, the McGraw-Hill Publishing Co. conducted a study among salespeople earning $50,000 or more annually (back when that was a lot of money). One of the questions they were asked was whether they actually asked for the order at the point of sale. Nearly 50 percent admitted they didn't do so, because they were ashamed to ask people for money.

Those findings surprised me, and they must have surprised plenty of others as well. Think about that. Here were people making their living selling products and services, but when the moment of truth came, they couldn't follow through. So many opportunities lost—and so many careers destined for mediocrity.

The irony of these facts has stayed with me through the years, and occasionally I've used it when talking to sales groups. What caught my attention most was the part about sales professionals not asking for the order because they were ashamed to ask others for money. That's how they perceived their jobs, and they didn't like it.

The McGraw-Hill survey came to mind again when I read an article in the *Wall Street Journal* about people and their money. According to the article, it seems there are a growing number of therapists treating people for "money neurosis." More and more of us are turning to psychologists, psychiatrists, and others to get over our money hang-ups. The article quotes several of them. One, David Krueger, a psychiatrist who treats financial disorders, puts it this way: "Money, along with food and sex, are the most common places where emotional issues hitchhike."

It's interesting how people perceive money. Some associate it with power, security, and even glamour, while others think of it as distasteful and dirty, something to be shunned.

165

Robert R. Butterworth, a clinical psychologist, puts a pragmatic perspective on how we relate to money. He says money may not be the No. 1 cause of marital disharmony, but in most cases it's in the top three.

Then there's the viewpoint of Christopher Mogil, whose specialty is working with people who've inherited wealth. He said one of his clients had inherited $100 million and was actually ashamed of his wealth. Mr. Mogil puts an ironic twist on money matters: "People who don't have enough money or have too much feel the same things. If you have a huge amount, you feel you have too many choices. If you have no money, you have no choices. Both feel paralyzed."

In the opinion of Arlene Matthews, a money counselor, the problems people have with money change with the times. For instance, in the 1980s, the message was buy, buy, buy. But in the '90s, the message is save, save, save. Her premise is that group thinking often determines how people relate to money.

Meanwhile, Olivia Mellan, a money therapist, has determined that there are seven types of patients who have problems with money: hoarders, spenders, money monks (who think money is evil and corrupt), money worriers, money amassers (who want to collect a lot of it), risk takers, and risk avoiders (who want financial safety and security above all else).

Money means different things to different people. I guess that's part of what makes the human species so interesting. But if you're in sales and haven't learned how to ask for the order, you probably won't have to worry about money—except that you're not likely to have very much of it.

Money isn't everything, but it sure helps pay the bills.

Profiles
in sales and
marketing excellence

67
Profile of
Frederick Foulston Lauer:
A salesman's salesman

 MY DAD, FREDERICK FOULSTON LAUER, was a salesman. In fact, he was a salesman's salesman. He loved his work. To give you an idea of how close he was to his clients, my first and middle names—Charles Spicer—are those of Charlie Spicer, my dad's best customer in Columbus, Ohio. My dad was the kind of individual people loved instinctively. He was someone you could trust, and he was someone with whom you could share your troubles. He was everything I ever wanted to be, and that's why I went into sales. What a role model he was.

Before he died of lung cancer in the late 1960s, my father gave me three pieces of advice that I well remember. First, I must always keep my word. That was important to him and should be to anyone who's in sales. A person's reputation and integrity are critically important in any walk of life. Then he emphasized that once I married, I should stay married. He believed in loyalty and believed that marriage was not to be taken lightly. He also reminded me that the world doesn't owe me or anyone else a living. In other words, make your own way, and don't look for a free ride.

Nothing fancy, nothing clever, and certainly nothing very intellectual. Just three pieces of commonsense advice from a salesman.

I'll always remember the times Dad took me with him to visit his clients. This was while I was home on vacation for a few days from college. He was the Eastern and Atlantic export manager for the Cribben & Sexton Co., which manufactured and sold Universal gas ranges. In those days, Universal was the Cadillac of the stove business. When we walked into an appliance store, my dad was always greeted by the salesmen on the floor. They were the ones who sold the Universal ranges, and he knew them all by name. He would listen to their problems as well as their jokes. Later, we would go to the back of the store, where the owner would always give my father an order for more stoves. It seemed to happen that way whenever I was with him—he always got an order.

Something else I noticed about my dad was the way he treated other people. For instance, he always treated taxi drivers, bellhops, doormen, and waiters with respect and courtesy. In return, they gave him good service. He tipped well and often told me he couldn't stand cheapskates—those individuals who are reluctant to pick up a check and who throw nickels around like manhole covers.

With women, he was always a gentleman. It was the way he helped them on with their coats and the way he always held the door open for them. Today it would probably be considered old-fashioned, but I still do those things and more, because I was taught that way by a true salesman.

Finally, my dad taught me how lucky I am to be a citizen of the United States. He considered it a distinct privilege to be an American, and he was proud of it. Like most Americans, he was generous, he was forgiving, and he was loyal to a fault.

I was so lucky to have him as my dad, and I miss him very much. I loved being with him, because he was fun to be with. He was proud of me, and I was very proud of him. He was the greatest salesman I ever knew, and I've tried to follow his advice as best I can. I'm still married to the same lady I wed more than thirty-five years ago. I try not to make promises I can't keep, and I, too, am proud of this great nation of ours and the opportunity to make my own way.

God bless America, God bless my father, and God bless the legacy he gave me.

68
Profile of Marty Sokoloff:
A haberdasher who cares

 PEOPLE COME INTO OUR LIVES from different directions, and we are so much richer for having encountered them. One particular good friend was one of the best salesmen I ever met. He epitomized selling, and if you could have watched him perform as I did, up close, you would have been most impressed. He exuded sincerity, and his approach was simple and straightforward.

The late Marty Sokoloff was a haberdasher. He sold clothing in my hometown for a retail outlet called Fell's that's one of my favorite places to buy shirts, socks, and suits, and that's where Marty sporadically entered my life. I usually saw him on the occasional weekend when I needed an article of clothing, and that's when we got the chance to talk.

Whenever I entered the store, Marty's greeting usually went something like this: "Chuck, how are you? How is Randy [my son] doing? And how's that grandson of yours? If he's anything like his dad, he's terrific! By the way, I'm glad you came by, because I've laid away a couple of suits for you that I think you would look great in. Let's try them on." I would usually offer token resistance, but I just love to be sold, and the way Marty handled me was a thing of beauty. He knew how to make a person feel special.

Now, I'm not a spendthrift, I'm not a clotheshorse, and I wasn't born with a silver spoon in my mouth, but if I told you how many suits and sports jackets I have in my closet, you would think I'm some sort of Beau Brummell. Sure, I've spent too much, and I've even had to sneak a suit or two into the house so my wife wouldn't catch on. But I always enjoyed doing business with

Marty, because I knew he got commissions on everything he sold and because he became such a dear friend.

For instance, when my book *Soar With the Eagles* was published, I did a book-signing in a store close to where Marty worked. Guess who was the first one to show up? Marty Sokoloff. Not only did he come by, but he also brought along five or six buddies and made sure each of them bought a copy of my book. Again, he made me feel like I was a pretty special person, and he went out of his way to do so.

Every so often, when I hadn't dropped by the store to see Marty, there would be a message on the answering machine at home: "Hi, Chuck. It's Marty at Fell's, and because I haven't seen you for a while I'm calling just to make sure everything is OK. Nothing important, but we all miss you here." How about that? Here was somebody who thought enough of me to make sure everything was all right just because I hadn't been around the store lately. That was Marty—thoughtful, caring, and always concerned.

I don't know where Marty learned how to sell, but he could have sold anybody anything, because he knew the secret behind every great salesperson—caring about his customers and letting them know how much they meant to him. It means taking nothing for granted and always making sure you stay in touch. It means good manners and remembering the little things such as birthdays, anniversaries, and children's names. And it means always keeping your customers in your heart.

Marty was music to my heart.

69
Profile of Mike Frost:
Overcoming doubts and fears

 I SUBSCRIBE TO A MONTHLY MAGAZINE titled *Selling* published by Capital Cities/ABC in New York. I enjoy the publication, because it talks about the things most salespeople deal with day in and day out. It's filled with all kinds of pointers, and it chronicles the success stories of people who have risen through the ranks. It also gives me a strong dose of enthusiasm and inspiration, which is why I look forward to each issue.

I was skimming through the June 1994 issue and by chance noticed a photo of a gentleman in a wheelchair. Over the weekend, I kept thinking about that picture. When I returned to the office on Monday and read that man's story, I was filled with nothing but admiration for his courage and determination.

His name is Mike Frost, and he was identified in the article as a salesman for MCI in Atlanta. According to the article, Mr. Frost had actually died in a surfing accident in 1982 at the age of twenty-two, but heroic attempts by his rescuers brought him back to life. Unfortunately, the accident paralyzed him from the neck down, and his future looked bleak indeed. At the time of the accident, he was a supervisor at a California home for the mentally challenged. When he got out of rehabilitation, he knew he had to make a career change. He moved back to his home state of Georgia and got a job as a telemarketer with MCI. For an ordinary person, that probably would be the end of the story, but not for Mike Frost. In 1987, he made the decision to try outside sales.

With the help of a customized van, which included a wheelchair lift and hand controls he could maneuver with the limited use of his arms he had regained, Mike Frost was ready to go...except for one major psychological hurdle—the fear of rejection. That's something all of us worry about from time to time, but for people in sales, it's experienced just about every day. Mike put it this way: "It was difficult at first because of my own fear of getting in front of the customer. I felt like the customer wasn't listening to what I had to say, because they had never been approached by someone in a wheelchair. But I came to realize that all salespeople experience rejection and that you can't take it personally."

In 1992, Mr. Frost was the top performer in MCI's Atlanta branch, earning six figures as a senior account executive. But selling isn't the only thing he does. Far from it. In his spare time he helps the disabled prepare to enter the work world and serves as the regional director for a youth training organization. He also offers peer support at a local spinal injury treatment center.

His philosophy of life is simple but to the point: "Since the day of the accident, I have lived by saying, 'Success is not being the best but doing your best.'"

Just think what Mike Frost has been able to accomplish. Think what it must be like for him just to get up in the morning, let alone report to a job filled with stress and rejection. Think what he has overcome to develop his positive attitude so that he can be successful. Yet, from time to time, I hear people complaining about their sinuses or the weather or other trivial matters, using them as an excuse to stay home from work or not to give their very best effort. Life is too precious to waste a single day, no matter what the reason. Success takes courage, discipline, and a positive attitude. That's never easy, but winners find a way to overcome their doubts and fears.

Here's a guy who had so much stacked against him, but he didn't give up. He didn't retreat into self-pity and certainly didn't become a recluse. He persevered, worked hard, and learned to deal with rejection. Mike Frost is a true champion, because he had the guts and determination to make sure nothing got in his way.

The next time you're down in the dumps or feel fatigued, think about the likes of Mike Frost. That should give you all the inspiration you need to get out there and excel.

173

Keeping the customer:
SUCCESS IN
CUSTOMER SERVICE

· ·

"People want to be treated with courtesy and respect
and like they're someone special, which they are!
Treat someone right today, and he or she will be back
tomorrow. Treat someone badly, and you might not get
a second chance."

WHY would any business or organization go out of its way to alienate its customers? Why would it treat them with contempt or indifference? That customers are the lifeblood of commerce is axiomatic. Yet many who market products or services treat their customers with insulting condescension and provide a generally abysmal and shabby level of service.

Enlightened companies know that satisfied, even delighted, customers are the key to growth and profits. By treating their customers with dignity and by giving them more than expected, such businesses thrive.

The essence
of
stellar customer service

70
Hold the spices
and stick to basic ingredients

 AS WITH ANYTHING important in life, you've got to practice it every day. There's no complicated formula, and there shouldn't be any mystery to it. I'm talking about sticking to the basics of your job or business. But too often that isn't what's happening. It becomes so tempting to do other things to spice up the routine a little, but that can lead to disaster. It happens because people forget what matters and forget what business they're in.

For a business to succeed in today's competitive world, there has to be a well-defined mission. We've all heard three words over and over—mission, vision, and values. Fundamental stuff, but it's anything but basic when individuals become bored or confused about where they're headed.

That's why so many businesses and individuals founder and fail. They haven't established a philosophy of doing business. "Keep it simple" comes to mind. That should be the motto of every member of the organization, from the chief executive on down.

Why do we need to continually remind ourselves about this? Because there are so many opportunities. But many companies and organizations run the risk of being shut out, because they've forgotten their core business. Remember, that's what got you where you are, and that's what you do best. Those basic ingredients have been your recipe for success so far, so stick with them. It's when you start to stray from your expertise that the trouble begins. I've seen it happen so many times.

Taking care of one's customers will never go out of style. However, I've attended too many meetings and seminars recently where I've heard all sorts of proposals about how to cut costs and deliver a product without any mention of the ultimate recipient. I understand some of the reasons for that, but the customer must always be an integral part of any discussion. Maybe we're confused, and maybe we've forgotten some of the basic lessons of staying in business. Or just maybe the customers don't mean much to us anymore because we've been taking them for granted.

I was taught to cater to customers, because they're the life-blood of any business. I also was taught to take care of their needs every day, not just once in a while. So my message is simply to get back to the reason you and your organization are in business—before you do anything else.

Companies that understand their mission and have sold their employees on that philosophy will do well. But companies that are all over the place and don't help their people stay focused on the mission are in for tough times. Yes, these are interesting times and changing times, but complicating things isn't the way to go. Choose simplicity.

71
Make service a way of life*

 I WAS MOVED when I read management consultant Tom Peters's syndicated column featuring a tribute to Leslie, a receptionist who works at his firm. How many of us would take the time to write a column or article or even a letter about a receptionist? Yet it's often the receptionist who will make or break a relationship with a customer or business contact.

What about your organization? Where are your Leslies? Do

---

* This piece is excerpted and adapted from a speech cowritten by Charles S. Lauer and Joyce Flory and originally presented by Mr. Lauer at a luncheon of chief operating officers in 1995.

they make sure callers talk to the right person? Do they take the initiative and solve the caller's problems? Are they what Peters calls the "one-person cheerleaders for life"?

Being around Leslie made Tom Peters realize something that's easy to forget when we're developing fish bone diagrams or using the latest TQM tool: "the enormous difference one person can make in the spirit of an organization…that energy and enthusiasm really are everything and have little to do with job title…and [that] the receptionist is probably the most important person in your organization."

Who's on the front line of your organization? Are they people such as Leslie, who—no matter what seems to happen—can always find the rainbow? Or are they just collecting a paycheck?

Most of us know that we're not running five-star hotels and resorts. And personally, I don't think that service happens just because you tell an employee to be nice or help people out. It takes systems, and it takes training. And sometimes organizations just haven't invested enough in it.

But there are still things we can learn from people such as the one-time concierge of the year at the Four Seasons Hotel in Washington, D.C., who summed up his job simply: "We just try to keep everyone happy."

72

Show your customers you care

NOT LONG AGO I purchased two window air conditioners and was told by the salesman that I could pick them up the following week, because they had to be shipped from another store. So there I was, standing on the floor of this giant retail/merchandising operation, looking for the salesman who had sold me the units. He was nowhere to be found, so I walked around to see if I could locate him. Eventually I found another salesperson and asked her whether the man who sold me the units was working that day. Her response: "He's not here, and anyway, it isn't my department."

I had unknowingly wandered into the refrigerator section, which was adjacent to the air conditioner section. I eventually found my salesman, but I couldn't forget what the saleswoman had said to me in a rather gruff way. Four words should be stricken from the business lexicon: *That's not my department.* What a shame when one person's offhand comments can mar the reputation not only of the company that's paying her salary but also of her sales colleagues.

Unfortunately, I really don't think this kind of behavior is just an occasional blip. I run into too many examples of shoddy customer service every day for that to be the case. For instance, I've just finished paying off a four-year car lease and have been toying with the idea of buying the vehicle. I've taken care of the car as though it were my own and consequently have developed a fondness for it. So I called the leasing firm to tell them what I wanted to do. That's when the waiting began.

I dialed the firm's toll-free number and was immediately informed by a recording that all representatives were busy. I was asked to wait, which I did. I waited and waited, the time interspersed with assurances—from another recording—that somebody would be with me shortly. Needless to say, it never happened. A few days later I tried again, but the same thing happened. It was frustrating, it was rude, and it was just plain bad business. Eventually I did get through, but it took a lot of effort and patience, and it left a bad taste in my mouth.

Here's another: In New York, I got caught in a meeting that was going to take longer than expected. So I called my airline in an attempt to make a flight change. But instead of the usual recording asking me to hang on until an agent could help me, I got a busy signal. I called several more times, all with the same result, so I was forced to go to the airport and take my chances on getting a flight back to Chicago. Everything worked out, but it was still frustrating. Again, it left me with a bad taste.

181

Now, these three little episodes really aren't a big deal, but they involve three of the biggest corporations in the United States today, all recognized as great companies that are customer oriented. Well, you couldn't convince me.

A lot of companies like to tell you how much they care. It sounds good, and the commercials are appealing, but all too often these firms drop the ball at the moment of truth. Quality customer service is serious business. Companies have to deliver.

Service isn't something that should be skimped on simply to save a few dollars here or there. If a customer calls to place an order, there should be someone there to take the call—immediately. Just think of the mentality of people who would put a paying customer on hold or maybe even ignore them, all in the name of saving a few bucks.

Quality service starts at the top. If the boss believes in customer service, then money will be spent on training and adequate staffing to do the job. But if management considers customers nuisances or mere numbers on a page, customer service deteriorates. So will business, and so will profits, I guarantee.

People want to be treated with courtesy and respect and like they're someone special, which they are! Treat someone right today, and he or she will be back tomorrow. Treat someone badly, and you might not get a second chance.

73

Customers prize good manners

THE SUBJECT OF GOOD MANNERS preoccupies me from time to time, so when I happened to turn on the car radio one day, I was more than interested in an interview with someone whose voice sounded familiar but whom I couldn't identify. This individual talked for a long time about how he deplores the kinds of bad manners he sees displayed these days by both adults and youngsters. He even claimed one of the major problems facing us as a society today is that too many parents don't take time to teach their children good manners. At the end of the interview, the announcer identified the man as the legendary golfer Arnold Palmer. Now, I don't know what made Mr. Palmer sound off on the issue, but what he had to say made a lot of sense to me, and it should concern all of us who consider ourselves members of a civilized society.

I see bad manners displayed almost everywhere I go, but it's especially shocking when I see such behavior by people in service businesses. They're often curt, uncaring, and just plain offensive. Sometimes I don't think they have a clue to what a customer's needs are. Frankly, I don't think a lot of them care, simply because they haven't been taught what's right and what's wrong in customer service.

The other sad part of the equation is that many companies—including service companies—don't make manners a high priority. The bottom line is important, but the people who run these organizations can't see beyond the ends of their noses. If they had true vision, they'd realize that happy customers will come back again and again, but unhappy customers will simply walk away.

All of us have been around people who practice good manners. Such individuals always stand out. And that's one of the secrets of success. If you really want to distinguish yourself in today's competitive marketplace, start putting heavy emphasis on treating customers with dignity and respect. You'll be amazed at the results. Basic things such as saying please and thank you are just the beginning.

The practice shouldn't be confined only to individuals; it should be standard corporate culture for any organization that truly wants to be outstanding, but it has to begin at the top. Unfortunately, too many of the so-called macho CEOs we read about so often are basically rude people. They think of themselves as "get-it-on" executives who can do just about anything with impunity, including treating people badly. But they come off as arrogant, self-absorbed brutes, and arrogance is one of the things we should decry in our leaders. Such executives almost invariably lead their companies into failure, because they simply don't care about others.

I can't emphasize the importance of good manners enough, whether it's in one's personal life or in the business world. Yes, there are abrasive, uncaring individuals, and there are companies completely lacking in genuine customer service. But we shouldn't tolerate such people, and we shouldn't do business with such companies.

The answer to all this is a renewed commitment to teaching good manners. There are organizations today that spend time instructing their employees in how to treat customers even when the customers are rude and abrasive themselves. And yes, there are parents who take the time to teach their children manners and respect, how to say yes, sir, and no, ma'am, and how to be deferential to people in authority, such as teachers and police officers. Such teachings should be universal.

So my message is this: There are so many poor-service companies and so many ill-mannered individuals today that if you practice good old-fashioned manners, you and your company will truly stand out.

74
Outstanding service
makes the world your oyster

 QUALITY CUSTOMER SERVICE is something I'm sure we all believe in and strive to practice. It's a must if you and your company are to be successful, no matter what business you're in. A lot of it, of course, is

intertwined with a good attitude. That positive attitude will show in many ways, but outstanding customer service tells the tale. With it, the world can be your oyster. Without it, any business is eventually doomed to failure.

Many businesses that in the past paid little attention to caring for the customer are now beginning to wake up and realize the value of standout service. My interest definitely was piqued when I came across an article in the *Chicago Tribune* chronicling an example—namely, the efforts of the towing industry to give its service reputation a lift.

Most of us have had this experience: The battery goes dead or the car breaks down, and there we are on the side of the road waiting for somebody to come along and help us. Of course, a phone call usually has to be made to get a tow truck dispatched. That can be traumatic, but the industry is working to make these encounters as painless as possible.

What took place at the National TowExpo 94 should be encouraging. Donna Bookout-Coe, a towing business owner and industry consultant from Portland, Oregon, conducted seminars at the annual conference sponsored by the Towing and Recovery Association of America (TRAA). One of her seminars was titled "Improving Your Roadside Manners." Ms. Bookout-Coe's message was simple: "Assuage, sympathize, and empathize….The whole thrust is to professionalize." She urged drivers to carry business cards, wear uniforms, and use gloves to keep their hands grease free. "They have to garner confidence immediately" whenever working with a stranded motorist, she said.

According to Jack Gratzianna, TRAA's president at the time of TowExpo 94, diffusing the anxiety of motorists is one of the highest priorities of the association's members—and it's a lesson being reinforced through a continuing education campaign by the trade group. Mr. Gratzianna says the average motorist needs a tow twice in a lifetime, and the tow truckers "have to be sensitive to that and not abuse someone already in a stressful situation."

The *Tribune* article notes that there's even a mobile wrecker's Hall of Fame, which is housed in a semitrailer. One of the members is Esa Pyyhkkalainen, a Finnish tow truck owner who was attending his fifth TowExpo. He owns a fifty-truck fleet in Finland and three vehicles based in neighboring Estonia. So towing is big business both here and abroad, and service is a key component.

There's nothing sophisticated here, just truckers using plain old common sense in making customers feel better. My point is this: Whether you're in towing or meat cutting or health care, the customer's needs and wants should be uppermost in your mind. While all companies claim to value their customers, in reality many give quality service short shrift. Well, taking the customer for granted is the easiest way to go out of business. It happens every day, and that's why there's so much opportunity out there.

You may be skeptical about a bunch of tow truck drivers trying to buff up their image by practicing improved customer service. That's because some of us have had truly nightmarish experiences with tow truckers. But there are a lot of dedicated professionals patrolling our roads. Maybe they can teach the others a lesson when it comes to service.

The next time your car breaks down and the tow truck driver gives you a smile while addressing you as sir or ma'am, and even wears gloves, don't laugh. You're probably in good hands.

75
A lesson in caring from Merck's vet

I'M SURE ALL OF US can tell stories about good customer service as well as bad customer service.

Something happened to me in 1991 that epitomized truly caring customer attention. And it all has to do with a dog—more specifically, a ten-year-old Alaskan malamute named Merck. He weighs 115 pounds, and for the past few years he and I have been close friends. Let me tell you

Merck's story, because it nicely illustrates what taking care of the customer is all about.

For several weeks I had noticed that Merck was having trouble moving about. It's hard to explain, but I'd noticed that he was rather stiff-legged when we went for a run or a walk. He just hadn't been himself.

Everything came to a head when Merck wasn't able to get up to go out for a walk with me. He seemed alert enough, and his tail wagged, but he just couldn't get up. Usually when he hears me getting his collar and leash, he makes a mad dash for the door, with tail wagging and plenty of body language to tell me he can't wait to get going. But that wasn't the case this time, and I was really concerned.

I called a veterinarian I had heard about—new to the area—who was trying to build his practice. This was his response: "From what you've told me, that dog should be seen as soon as possible. It could be anything, maybe even a disk. It would be better to see him here, because I can take some x-rays. But if you need me to come there, I have a station wagon and a stretcher, and we can get him back here for a thorough examination."

That's all I needed to hear. I drove to the new vet's office and got the stretcher. With the help of a neighbor, we got Merck into my Blazer. And guess what happened? As soon as Merck got into the car, he stood up. And when we got to the vet's office, he was even able to get out all by himself and walk into the doctor's office.

What happened next was a real lesson in caring. Dr. Barry Miller, this veterinarian I had never met before, checked Merck for more than an hour and took some x-rays. What it all boiled down to was that Merck had a fused disk in his back, which can cause problems with his spinal cord from time to time. It's not life-threatening, and with some weight loss, a couple of aspirin every once in a while, and some moderation in his exercise program, he should live a happy life over the next few years. The gentleman who made this diagnosis explained everything to me with the help of diagrams and textbooks. I was impressed. And I was relieved. I made the decision right then about who my veterinarian was going to be.

From an everyday event like this, we can learn so much. Sometimes we are so busy that we forget what we are in the business of doing—*listening and taking care of our customers.* Their every whim should be a signal to leap into action no matter how trivial their desires and needs seem to be.

Always remember that customers are like you and me. If you don't pay close attention, you may lose a long-time customer simply because you didn't take the time to really care.

76
Merck: The sequel

 AS I WRITE THIS, summer's almost over, and as far as I'm concerned, it can't end fast enough. That's because I'm a cold-weather person. Hot and humid weather gets me down, but when there's a chill in the air, I feel invigorated. So I'm looking forward to fall and winter. But I want to share something that happened earlier this summer, and it has to do with Merck, my big Alaskan malamute.

Merck is probably the most handsome dog I've ever seen. My son, Randy, gave him to me before shipping out to the Far East while in the U.S. Marine Corps. Actually, Merck was given to me on loan, but when my son returned stateside about a year later, he could see that the two of us had formed a pretty close bond, and, consequently, he let me keep Merck. And what a godsend Merck has been. I have had unbelievable adventures with him, and he's everything you could want in a dog—a loyal, affectionate, constant companion.

Merck's background story goes like this. When my son was stationed at the Marine base in Twentynine Palms, California, he was shaving one morning, when he noticed a dog outside reflected in the mirror. He immediately was struck by the dog's bearing and his beautiful coat, and he assumed the dog belonged to a neighbor. But that wasn't the case, because Merck kept hanging around the house my son shared with some other Marine Corps officers. Eventually, Randy took Merck in. He tried to find the owners by advertising through the local newspaper and radio stations, and by checking with the local shelter. This went on for three months, but no one came forward to claim Merck.

One of the sad facts of military life is that when servicemen and -women are transferred overseas, their pets aren't allowed in some countries. And because the military makes no provision for pets, sometimes their owners simply turn them loose and let them fend for themselves. I can't believe anyone could have done that to Merck, but if they did, they sure gave away something special.

So the years with Merck have been great, but lately he has been having some health problems. Nothing really major, but one episode scared me. Near the end of my vacation in Minnesota, we were taking our normal walk along the lakeshore, when Merck experienced a seizure.

He came out of it after a brief period, and I rushed him to the local veterinarian, who felt he should have some tests and be placed in observation. I wanted to get him back to my vet in Chicago, who knew Merck and his history. So that afternoon, Merck and I drove straight through to Chicago, about twelve hours. The next morning I was in the vet's office. He was kept for a couple of days and prescribed some medication that he has been taking for the past two weeks.

Things seem to be improving, but the doctors still are trying to pinpoint the problem with all kinds of tests. Hopefully, all of this will end up OK. I know my vet—Dr. Barry Miller—is doing everything he can, and then some, to get Merck back to being his old self.

I had taken Merck to the vet's office on a Thursday, and after he was observed for a couple of days, I was allowed to take him home for the weekend. I was nervous, because the doctor still hadn't been able to figure out what caused the seizure. But before I left the veterinarian's office, Dr. Miller did something I'll always remember. He gave me his beeper number and told me that if anything happened to my dog, he wanted me to call him. Here's a guy who works six days a week, and he's telling me to interrupt him even on his day off if I need him for any reason. Later, an associate from his office called me several times to check on Merck. Talk about customer service! Here are staff members who not only are dedicated to their jobs but who also know how to allay the fears of their customers.

I call Dr. Miller the "beeper doctor." He's working hard to build a new veterinary practice, and with the caring, committed service he has shown, I know he'll continue to succeed. It's what customer service is all about. Call it what you will—follow-through, going beyond the call of duty, commitment—it all has to do with attitude. And good service is good attitude.

There's nothing fancy, no secret formula here. Good service is just treating people (and in this case, animals) well. Dr. Miller is special because he treats people and animals with special care.

Avoiding
black
holes

77

The "moment of truth" in customer service

IT HAPPENED at the Tampa airport. It's really no big deal, but it does demonstrate a mentality that spells mediocrity, maybe even failure.

I had arrived at Tampa from Chicago and was at a rental car counter arranging for a car to drive to a CEO conference. I was headed for a place called Innisbrook, a resort about an hour from the Tampa airport. I'm always in a slightly confused state when I get off a flight, and even though I had a general idea of where I was going, I asked the car rental agent if she could give me directions to Innisbrook. That's when she pointed to a machine and said, "Use that," and then, practically in the same breath, asked the next customer to step forward.

I was miffed. I'm not good with computers and machines I don't know how to operate, so it took me quite a while to figure everything out and get my directions. While I was trying to figure out the machine, the rental agent didn't pay any attention to me. It was fairly obvious that she didn't care. Think about that—she just didn't care.

Now, maybe the rental car business has escaped all the competitive pressures the rest of us face every day, but I don't think that's the case. Maybe some employees think customers aren't important, but I'll bet you the top person at that rental agency would be upset by how I was treated in Tampa that day. The rental agent was really efficient as she went about her business of getting me a car, but by treating me in such a cavalier manner, she left me with a negative impression.

192

That's what is known as a "moment of truth"—when someone from the company is dealing with a customer. Today, with so many companies vying for the same customers, it's the details that make the difference. Little blips of rudeness can destroy a sale and a relationship.

Why the problem? It's simple. People aren't being trained to pay attention to details when they deal with customers. Rudeness has become a way of life in the service business. Many service employees are treated rudely by their supervisors and aren't paid very well for their hard work. Studies show, however, that despite the low salaries, employees will go out of their way to help customers if they're trained to do so and if they're treated well by their own companies.

Employees must know that the little things can make a big difference—things such as answering the telephone with enthusiasm and asking people how you can help them, and then following through by going the extra distance to take care of the customer. It's also saying how much you appreciate a person's business. Believe me, customers remember good service, and they'll come back.

Many people say they feel like servants when they have to help someone or wait on tables, or whatever they must do to serve their customers, but those are the people who keep a business going. Don't be ashamed to cater to your customers' needs. This is what separates the winners from the losers. Don't treat telephone calls as interruptions and let the phone ring and ring. It could be a customer trying to get through, either to place an order or to ask a question. Either way, it's a chance to make contact with the lifeblood of any business—the customer.

Customers are just like you and me. They have needs and wants, and more often than not, they need someone to help them. What an opportunity to make an impression. Look around you and see which businesses are thriving, and you'll find the common denominator is good service. At those companies, nothing is too good for the customer.

Wake up, ladies and gentlemen. There are lots of rude people out there turning customers off. Don't be one of those individuals, and don't be one of those companies. Good manners, common sense, and a willingness to take that extra step will make the difference. If you sense there's a problem at your organization, start working with your people today. But begin by treating *them* with dignity and respect.

78

Place yourself in your customer's shoes

IN THE EARLY '90s, when certain banks started giving customers a $5 bill if they had to wait in line longer than five minutes, a lot of people could hardly believe it. But that's exactly what some banks did to make sure their customers were given compensation for any inconvenience caused by a lengthy wait. And to me, that made all the sense in the world. Let me explain.

One of my biggest pet peeves is this: Too many businesses really don't seem to care about the inconvenience they often cause their customers. Think how important time is to everyone today; there never seem to be enough hours in a day. We seem to be running just to stay even. People are continually looking for businesses that care about convenience, and they're even willing to pay more for it. This was borne out by a study conducted by the research firm Cambridge Reports. The study showed that three out of every five people surveyed said that in choosing a service, cost is less important than having needs met. But it's incredible the number of businesses that still don't get the message.

Robert B. Tucker, author of *Managing the Future* (Putnam, 1991), believes there are simple questions that management can ask to determine if an organization is truly addressing the fundamentals of catering to the customer: Is it easy to order your product or service? Is service personalized? Are your customers dealing with people who seem to care, and know what they're talking about? Do you make appointments for delivery so customers don't have to waste a whole day waiting? Are the hours convenient?

George Conomikes, one of the nation's top physician practice management consultants, told me a story that demonstrated both convenience and caring by an automobile dealership. Mr. Conomikes said that he had never bought a foreign car before, but decided to get a Honda as a second vehicle. It bothered him, he said, that when he took his American car to the local dealership for service, he was routinely told to leave it for the whole day, even if it was only for a lube and oil change.

On the other hand, much to his surprise, when he took his new Honda in for an oil change, he was told the car would be finished in forty-five minutes at most. And when he did get his car back—within forty-five minutes as promised—it also had been washed. He was told it was standard practice at the dealership to wash all cars that were serviced, no matter how minor the service or repairs. Think about it. The dealership used a simple thing like a car wash to make the customer feel special.

Go ahead and place yourself in the position of trying to do business with your company, and then ask yourself the questions posed earlier by Robert B. Tucker. Better still, call your company and try to place an order or just ask some questions about the company. You might be shocked.

Imagine, for example, calling your office to talk to one of your salespeople, finding none of them there, and being transferred to the corporate switchboard. After asking for the person by name, you're then put on hold.

In about thirty seconds, the operator comes back on the line to tell you that not only was the person you asked for not employed there, but that the company has no such department as the one you've asked for. It's hard to believe this actually happens, but I've heard true stories of similar exchanges many times.

What this all boils down to is that in an age when time and convenience are at a premium, it's extremely important to cater to the needs of customers. They're asking for and demanding high quality service, and when they don't get it, they go elsewhere.

Companies that realize this will prosper in the '90s, but those that don't will go out of business…simply because they've forgotten why they're in business—*the customer.*

79
When to schedule staff meetings

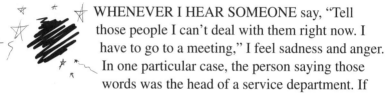 WHENEVER I HEAR SOMEONE say, "Tell those people I can't deal with them right now. I have to go to a meeting," I feel sadness and anger. In one particular case, the person saying those words was the head of a service department. If you think this type of thing doesn't happen often, think again; it's happening all the time in America. It's happening because service people still aren't being grounded in the basics of serving customers or, worse still, the boss thinks having meetings is more important than taking care of customers' needs. That kind of thinking will lead to disaster. There are companies falling by the wayside every day because they have forgotten that the purpose of any business is to take care of the customer *now*—not tomorrow, not next week, but today, this very minute.

I strongly believe that anyone involved in customer service shouldn't be going to meetings during regular business hours. The time for those meetings is early in the morning before business hours or at night after work. During the day, everyone should be poised to serve the needs of customers—immediately. It sounds so simple, doesn't it? But that philosophy isn't being followed at many of the companies I'm familiar with.

As a matter of fact, I know of a company where the person in charge of customer service spends more time in meetings than she spends on the job. That's because her boss thinks having meetings about customer service during working hours makes for better

196

service. But that becomes a catch-22 scenario. This individual is frustrating his employees, since they can't do their jobs (thanks to all the meetings), and he's also losing customers due to poor service.

The best meetings last two or three minutes. People stand. They don't sit, they don't sip coffee, they don't get comfy. They know they're there to resolve something or be told something, so they pay attention. It works, but not too many people have caught on.

Bureaucrats love meetings. They love to talk things over, because, as a rule, they don't have much else to do. It makes them feel as if they're doing something important, when the only thing they're really doing is wasting valuable time that should be spent taking care of customers. Such meetings go on and on.

Please don't get me wrong. I know some meetings have to last longer than a couple of minutes in order to resolve complicated negotiations or deal with other crucial matters. But if the individuals attending are in customer service, don't keep them too long. You didn't hire them to spend half the day sitting in meetings.

Meetings are seductive. It's kind of nice to schmooze with colleagues in a relaxed atmosphere. It's kind of nice to take a break from your real job and maybe even learn something. Remember, though, that while you're doing this, customers are calling. They often need attention from *you*, not your assistant, some part-timer, or a secretary—no matter how good these people are.

I'm not a meeting person. Frankly, I find most meetings to be a waste of time. That's because I don't believe employees should sit on their duffs when customers are out there who need to be cultivated, soothed, and helped. Any time you're invited to attend a meeting, ask why, and then find out if you can skip it. I'll say it's ten-to-one the meeting will be a waste of your time, even if you're not in customer service. You might just want to do something to improve the product line or something else that's more constructive.

Customers are the lifeblood of any business, so they should be the top priority of any organization that wants to stay in business. Meetings, bureaucracies, fancy titles, and political

197

infighting are for companies that are headed for failure. Leon Gorman of L.L. Bean says it best: "Service is a day-in, day-out, ongoing, never-ending, unremitting, persevering, compassionate type of activity."

The best meetings are with your customers.

80

Lauer at length: How automated communication can drive away your customers*

I WAS A SPEAKER at a 1992 conference sponsored by the management services division of IMS America for about 350 pharmaceutical salespeople, product managers, and information systems specialists. And as I listened to a number of presentations by other speakers, I was struck by the laughter and applause that followed a remark by one of the leading consultants in health care. It went something like this: "A friend of mine told me that voice mail offers you the opportunity, at the

---

* Sections of this piece are excerpted and adapted from a speech cowritten by Charles S. Lauer and Joyce Flory, and originally presented by Mr. Lauer at a luncheon of chief operating officers in 1995.

end of the workday, to listen to a number of business messages in the privacy of your home, almost all of which could have waited till the next day."

More recently, I spoke to the sales force of a top supplier in the health care industry. I discussed one of my favorite subjects: the importance of taking care of the customer. I reminded them that customers are the lifeblood of any enterprise. Without them, there's no reason to be in business.

In the course of my comments, I mentioned how frustrated I've become with voice mail and how I believe it's had a damaging effect on customer service. As soon as I said this, the roomful of salespeople burst out in applause, making it obvious they concurred. Frankly, I wouldn't have been able to back up my statement with any hard data if I had been asked to do so. It's simply my gut feeling; I guess you could say I'm old-fashioned. But if you really care about your customers and really care how they're treated when they call your company, I advise you to note carefully the information I'm about to share.

We've all experienced the frustration of listening to a message like this: "You have reached XYZ Company. No one is available to take your call at the moment, but press 1 for further options." You then enter the maze. If you have plenty of time, you may be willing to get involved in the button pushing game.

Then there's the bizarre scenario of being switched from one message box to another and, seemingly, not being able to get in or out. It's a process filled with frustration and idiocy. But, of course, we're told that voice mail is more efficient and less costly to an organization. So what if customers are inconvenienced? Here's what: We apparently share a lot of anger over our confrontations with voice mail.

In my opinion, if you're into customer service, and you truly believe customers are the lifeblood of your company, voice mail is not the way to go. But the systems are in use in a growing number of companies, so maybe customers aren't that important to them after all.

Now, so you don't get the wrong idea, I believe that in some cases there are practical and worthwhile applications for voice

199

mail. Automation has its place, but don't forget that customers are special. They are our reason for being. They spend money with us. They help make us profitable. They make it all happen. But we seem to have lost our way, even though there are more and more books and seminars being offered about good customer service and how customers should be treated. What's happened in many organizations is that individuals have become more concerned about their own convenience and comfort level, forgetting about the customer. They've forgotten why they're in business.

The moment of truth for any company is when a customer first tries to make contact. We're told the first impression is the one that will last forever. If customers are greeted by voice mail when they want to place an order, I believe many will simply hang up. They don't want to be handled as nonentities but as living, caring people treated with dignity and respect—just like you and me.

I think these automated systems in general smack of rudeness. Think about it. Let's say I call a company, but instead of hearing a live person on the line, I'm greeted by a recorded voice that tells me to press buttons for the appropriate department...and wait; or press another button to reach an operator...and probably wait some more. In short, buddy, wait in line with the others; you really aren't that important to us. That's the way the message is often understood, make no mistake about it.

We also may be sharing a big tab because of it. Northern Telecom, a prominent telecommunications company, completed a study that shows how ineffective voice mail can be. The findings were reported in July 1995 in the *Chicago Tribune*. According to the Northern Telecom survey, American business wastes nearly $3 billion a year listening and waiting and pushing buttons for options in voice mail systems. Employees spend an average of 302 hours a year listening to and responding to voice mail messages, the survey said. Almost three-fourths of the survey respondents claimed their jobs are affected by being unable to reach people on a timely basis. Some 78 percent said they were frustrated, and 58 percent claimed they were stressed.

But here's something to which every company should pay

close attention: Forty-five percent of the respondents said they took their business elsewhere when they were unable to contact their preferred supplier. Think what that could mean for any business. Yet there are still companies stepping over dollars to get to pennies. They're treating their customers rudely, committing the biggest sin of all.

I know there's a lot technology can give us. I don't know where *Modern Healthcare* would be if we didn't have access to services like the PR Newswire and Business Wire. And it's great to be getting E-mail via modem from our readers.

But the thing I always remember when I hear people talk about technology is a statement made by Harvard marketing guru Theodore Levitt. He said, "Data is not information. And information is not meaning."

What is he saying here? His message is simple: Just because you have reams of data doesn't necessarily mean that you have usable information. And just because you have information doesn't mean you've figured out what it means for your organization and your market.

Personally, I'd like to add a third piece to his statement: Information is not a relationship.

People insist that in the future more of our communication will be carried out electronically. Of course, some of that is terrific. But somehow, no matter how many computers we have, there's nothing that can take the place of one-on-one conversation.

Something special happens when two people—or five people—sit in a room, face to face. That something is called intimacy. It may be a doctor and a patient, a manager and an employee, two friends, or a married couple. But nothing can quite take its place.

So as we barrel down the information highway, let's not forget that sometimes it's OK if we stop, get out of our race cars, and travel on foot. And sometimes it's OK to travel on the side of the road, pulling our little red wagons. Speed isn't everything.

My advice is to take time to enjoy people—from the employees who work for you to the customers or clients you serve. A ten-minute conversation with a customer may tell you more about what's right and wrong with your organization than a $5,000 research study. What better way to find out what customers and employees really want than sitting down with them over a cup of coffee? I hope we never forget the healing power of face-to-face conversation.

I know we are in a new age. I realize computers and the magic they can bring about are supposed to take us to the promised land. I don't quibble with that thinking, but people still like to be treated with courtesy and respect when they are about to spend money with any business. This fact seems to be overlooked by too many companies that should know better.

Don't ever make people wait to spend money with you. Put yourself in their shoes. If you were about to place a big order, why should you have to deal with a machine that treats you just like everybody else and even makes you work to spend your money? That's certainly not customer service. Even more important, you could be losing business left and right and not even know it's happening.

Every sales-oriented company had better review its voice mail system—and then start over. Customers are everything. They deserve live and courteous treatment every time they call. Otherwise, the next call will probably be to a competitor.

A customer isn't someone to match wits with or someone to try to outsmart, but I can tell you many companies try to do just that with their sales brochures and their product pricing. In so many ways, customers are treated like nuisances or interruptions. One executive even said, "This would be a great business if it wasn't for the customers."

Maybe I'm just old-fashioned and the world is passing me by, but I was taught differently. I was taught to greet my customers personally, to take care of them, and to make sure I listened to their needs. When a customer calls, I want to be at the other end, offering to help in any way I can.

Profiles
in
customer service excellence

81
Profile of Roy Dyment:
Going the extra mile

 WE ALL HEAR STORIES from time to time that grab our attention. I love hearing about people who go the extra mile—people who are so enthusiastic about their jobs and life in general that they do special things that others wouldn't even consider doing. They're special individuals who deserve to be applauded.

When I think of such dedicated professionals, I'm reminded of Roy Dyment, a longtime doorman at the Four Seasons Hotel in Toronto, Ontario. His story is legendary and it goes like this: One day, a man exited the Four Seasons in a great hurry. He asked Dyment to hail a cab for him, which he did. An hour later, Dyment noticed the fellow's briefcase near the curb.

He immediately went to the bell captain to ask him to cover for him. Dyment called the man's office in Washington and talked to his secretary, who told him her boss was beside himself because he needed important papers that were in the briefcase. The secretary then asked Dyment to have a messenger take the briefcase to Washington as fast as possible.

Dyment went to his locker and changed clothes. He then headed to the airport and bought a round-trip ticket to Washington. Upon arrival, he personally delivered the man's briefcase and apologized to the startled attorney for his (Dyment's) mistake.

For sure, that's big-time customer service. For his efforts, Roy Dyment was named employee of the month by Four Seasons management. Later he was chosen employee of the year.

Such stories should inspire all of us to try harder and go out of our way for our prospects and our customers.

82

Profile of Frank Pacetta: A motivator extraordinaire shares his ten-point formula for success

HOORAY FOR FRANK PACETTA! He's a winner, a doer, a maverick. He's what you and I admire in a person: someone who believes in taking care of the customer. Just reading about him pumped me up. His story is what leadership is all about, and it's the difference between winning and losing. Frank Pacetta is strong-willed, opinionated, stubborn, and creative. He's a motivator extraordinaire.

The story about Mr. Pacetta, at the time a district sales manager for Xerox Corp. in Cleveland, appeared in the *Wall Street Journal*. The office that Mr. Pacetta took over was virtually in shambles when he stepped in. Things were so bad that people in the office didn't think anyone would be crazy enough to take the top job. But there stood Frank Pacetta, then thirty-three years old, telling what was left of the staff that the Cleveland district would finish the year No. 1 in the region—including eleven other districts—even though that district had finished last the previous year. Sure enough, risk taker, street fighter Frank Pacetta took his district not only to the No. 1 spot in the region but also to No. 4 among Xerox's sixty-five districts nationwide, as measured by how far the districts exceeded goals set by corporate headquarters.

How did he do it? He did it with good old-fashioned discipline and by paying attention to customer details. He did it by fighting the home office and all of the management-driven bureaucratic

205

policies formulated to make things convenient and orderly for the personnel at headquarters. Bureaucrats often forget that the troops on the front line are dealing with customers who need help and understanding, customers who in many cases are irascible and unpredictable. Bureaucrats simply forget what their jobs are all about—taking care of customers and making it easier for customers to do business with their company.

Frank Pacetta didn't make popularity his No. 1 goal. He emphasized dressing professionally, paying attention to such things as shined shoes and collars starched so well "that you can skate on them." They're basic things, but they're so important. He hired effectively, making sure he included women and other minorities on his sales force and paid and rewarded all his troops well. He gave them plaques for above-average performance. As he put it in the article, "When you're in sales, it's lonely and it's war, and you want to hear your name."

Frank Pacetta also used entertainment, such as golf outings and other social gatherings, to cement relationships with customers. According to the article, he always exceeded his expense budget but explained that he more than made up for it with increased sales.

Sources in the article said that since Mr. Pacetta took over, more than 70 percent of his fifty-seven-member staff had quit, moved to another district, or been fired. But the salespeople who remained under him, and the new hires, were winning more sales and making more money than they ever dreamed possible.

Just what was Mr. Pacetta's formula for success? He offered ten tenets:

1. Prepare customer proposals on evenings and weekends.
2. Never say no to a customer.
3. Make customers feel good about you, not just your products, by doing simple things such as taking them to lunch or to a ball game and sending them birthday cards.
4. Meet customer requirements, even if it means fighting your own bureaucracy.
5. Do things for customers you don't get paid for or that aren't your responsibility, such as solving billing problems.

6. Know your competitors' products better than your competitors do.
7. Be early for meetings.
8. Dress and groom yourself sharply so "you look like a superior product."
9. When it's time to go home, make one last telephone call.
10. If you stay in the shower a long time in the morning because you don't look forward to work, find another job.

You'd better believe it's a war out there. But if you follow these ten rules, there's no way you're going to lose. Vince Lombardi would have loved Frank Pacetta.

Nothing fancy, no secrets—just paying attention to the customer.

83
Profile of Nordstrom: Legendary service puts customers at the top

 IT'S A GREAT STORY that should energize anyone who deals with customers. It appeared in *Positive Impact*, a monthly newsletter that offers its readers a collection of articles on customer service. As the story goes, shortly after his wife died, a man called his local Nordstrom department store so he could settle his wife's account. She owed $1,000, and the husband simply wanted to clear the books. Over the years she had been a good customer. The husband was given the balance amount and then was asked why he needed the information. He replied that his wife had passed away. A couple of days later he received a letter from Nordstrom saying he should consider his wife's account paid in full. But that wasn't all. The day of her funeral, the store sent flowers.

Here's another example of Nordstrom's caring customer service. In early 1996, parts of the Northwest were hit by terrible flooding. Nordstrom customers in that region received a postcard with these words:

> We, at Nordstrom, are concerned for those of you living in the areas devastated by the floods in Washington, Oregon, and Idaho.
>
> We sincerely hope that you or your family have not been adversely affected.
>
> If you need to make special arrangements with us concerning your Nordstrom credit account, please write or call us...

That's big-time customer service. And it's the reason Nordstrom is legendary for doting on its customers. But there's much more to the Nordstrom story. The chain has the highest-paid sales staff in retailing, and it trains and upgrades its employees constantly. In other words, Nordstrom managers don't skimp when it comes to taking care of their workers. Caring for their people is mirrored in how those employees treat customers—and those things account for Nordstrom's success.

A review of the book *The Nordstrom Way: The Inside Story of America's #1 Customer Service Company* (Wylie and Sons, 1995), which appeared in the same issue of *Positive Impact*, gives a snapshot of Nordstrom employee dedication. The book's authors, Robert Spector and Patrick D. McCarthy, relate this incident: "One day a sales associate ran across the street to a competitor's store to purchase a pair of women's pants at full price in order to resell them to a Nordstrom customer at Nordstrom's sale price." Again, that's service above and beyond the call of duty.

The same review describes the unique way Nordstrom is organized. Picture an inverted pyramid, with customers positioned at the top. Just below them are employees (including sales and support people), followed by management and buyers. You'll find the board of directors at the very bottom.

Coauthor McCarthy has been Nordstrom's top salesperson for some twenty years. His base is a modest $9.85 per hour, but year after year he commands a six-figure salary because of his commissions. One of his secrets: He has more than six thousand names on his Rolodex. Apparently, he's selling all the time.

Customers want and need constant attention. Make sure you give it to them. If you want to succeed, you have no other choice.

And then some...

"We have the freedom to choose—every day—between kindness and cruelty, immediate reward and long-term gain, hope and despair.... But the No. 1 choice, the choice that determines all other choices, is the attitude and approach to living and business we choose for ourselves."

SOME people aspire only to achieve the minimum. They want to know how little they can do or give to "get by." Others, happily, always attempt to go that extra mile—to exceed the expected.

Those who give only what's required or requested end up short-changing themselves. In the workplace, they are rarely rewarded with raises and promotions. And in their relationships, they get back no more than they give.

People who keep charging forward long after others stop not only bless the world they live in but reap great personal and professional rewards. They do the job, "and then some." They go the distance, "and then some." They always add a little extra—and it is precisely that margin that vaults them past those who quit when the clock strikes five.

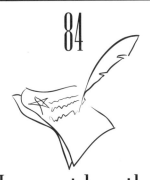

Lauer at length:
Let your attitude set your altitude*

A PROMINENT SALESMAN summed up his business success in three words: *and then some.* He told people that, at a very early age, he had discovered the difference between average people and top people.

■ The top people, he said, did what was expected of them—*and then some.*

■ They were thoughtful of others, they were considerate and kind—*and then some.*

■ They met their obligations and responsibilities fairly and squarely—*and then some.*

■ They were good friends to their friends—*and then some.*

■ They could be counted on in an emergency—*and then some.*

　　And then some. Three little words that could probably go a long way in transforming the government, business, even our society.

　　The nicest thing about the philosophy of *and then some* is that you don't have to spend a lot of money, execute a corporate turnaround, or come up with a breakthrough to practice it. *And then some* reflects the idea that little things mean a lot. Or, if you

---

* This piece is excerpted and adapted from a speech originally presented by Charles S. Lauer in January 1996 in Cleveland to Lake County Hospital System.

prefer an expression coined by another wise person: "Practice random acts of kindness and senseless beauty."

And then some—

■ Maybe it's a teenager leaving a room a little cleaner than it was before—even though that sounds like an impossible dream to those of us who've been parents.

■ Not just being a critic, but offering a few suggestions.

■ Closing a door that needs closing, cleaning a desk that needs cleaning, or helping someone who needs help—even though those things were never mentioned in your job description and even though some colleagues might think it's beneath you.

■ Not just giving someone directions, but actually taking the time to draw a map.

■ Not just speaking to someone, but leaving them with a handshake and a hug.

■ Not just smiling politely, but taking the time to speak a few kind words.

That's the philosophy of *and then some*—a great attitude matched by equally important but small actions.

Let me give you an example of what I mean. A lot of us like to pretend we don't read columns such as those produced by Ann Landers, but read them we do. Personally, I find she offers wonderful insights into what people are really thinking, plus some incredibly touching stories. In 1989 she ran this story: "Last Sunday I attended an art exhibit in Michigan. I was wandering around among hundreds of people when a young woman touched my arm and said, 'You are a beautiful lady.' Ann, I'm eighty-eight years old and never considered myself anything special to look at. But I'm healthy and happy and grateful to the good Lord for all my blessings. Every day, I've been cheered by that lovely compliment. It gave my heart a lift."

In a tiny way, a stranger had transformed that woman's life—if only for a week. But even more important, that simple act illustrates the notion that the attitude we bring to a situation is everything. To put it another way, attitude, not aptitude, determines where you'll end up and how people respond to you. Stated another way, attitude determines *altitude*—not just for your career, but for your community, your profession, and even for your country.

The great religious writer Charles Swindoll probably expressed it best when he said that "attitude is more important than facts, than the past, than education, than money, than circumstances, than failures, than successes, than what other people say or do. Attitude is more important than appearance or skill. It can make or break a company…a church…a home."

And other people seem to bear him out. In his great book *Learned Optimism* (Knopf, 1990), Martin Seligman went through hundreds of studies. The bottom line? People with a positive, optimistic attitude did better in love, at work, and on the playing field. When they ran for office, they were more apt to be elected. And they aged well and lived longer.

Attitude makes a difference in life—and it can make a difference for those in business. For example, we can choose to worry about tightening budgets or we can look for new opportunities we haven't uncovered yet. We can operate out of fear and anxiety and let other peoples' grim predictions shape our future, or we can let our positive attitude determine our altitude.

If you've felt victimized by what some people are saying about the future of your business—and your prospects for employment—you're not alone. You're keeping company with some of the great minds in history.

Who would have guessed that one of Abraham Lincoln's teachers once said, "When you consider Abe has had only four months of school, he's good at his studies. But he's a daydreamer and asks foolish questions."

Happily, Abe decided not to take that critique too seriously. His daydreaming paid off, and his thoughtful questions turned out not to be quite so foolish after all.

And then there was Woodrow Wilson, the man who guided the country through World War I. Fortunately, he never bothered to listen to his teacher's evaluation: "Woodrow is ten years old and is only just beginning to read. He shows signs of improving, but you mustn't set your sights too high."

And then, of course, there was Albert Einstein. You would

have thought that he—of all people—would have had it easy. But no such luck. Albert's poor parents got this report: "Albert is a very poor student. He's mentally slow, unsociable, and always daydreaming. He's spoiling it for the rest of the class and it would be in the best interests of all if he were removed from the school."

Of course, Albert did go on to fail his college entrance exams. But, as they say, the rest is history.

The point I'm making here is not that everyone should model their lives after Abraham Lincoln, Woodrow Wilson, or Albert Einstein. They lived different lives—and they lived in different times. In fact, today you wonder if they would have been diagnosed with attention deficit disorder.

My point is that no matter how old we get, negative types will always be out there. You know them—the people who are more than willing to issue a diagnosis, cut off your options, and make grim and grisly predictions about the future. Maybe they take the form of a legislator, an investment analyst, or a media pundit. But all of these people seem to have one thing in common: They seem to think they know it all—not just for the present, but for the short- and long-term future.

The one great thing we can learn from entertaining stories about people such as Lincoln, Wilson, Einstein, or any other kid who was pegged wrong, is that it pays to stand up to others. It pays not to let someone else decide your fate. And it pays to let your attitude—not somebody's judgments—set your altitude. With little more than a positive attitude, these people overcame their problems and proved their teachers wrong, the same way business and industry in this country has proved doom and gloom specialists wrong time after time.

And there's something else. Look at some of the greatest people in history and you'll discover that they overcame tremendous adversity extending way beyond a comment made by a well-meaning but overly critical teacher. Moses was supposed to have been a stutterer, St. Paul had epileptic fits, and Charles Darwin suffered one ailment after another for most of his adult life, right up until his dying day. Even Thomas Edison, F. Scott Fitzgerald, and, more recently, Cher, had learning disabilities. Yet all of them, in their own way, managed to make a contribution in their fields. Their attitude—not an outsider's diagnosis—determined their altitude.

I like to hark back to the career of Abraham Lincoln. Remembered in our hearts forever, this was a man who won only 25 percent of the time. If you consider what he went through, you realize why I keep saying that attitude sets the altitude. Lincoln could have given up in 1832 when he lost his job and an election, or when he lost his business a year later, or when the girl he loved died a year after that. He could have surrendered in 1838 and 1843 and 1854 when he lost elections. But Lincoln decided never to give up...and finally he was elected president in 1860. No one understood better than Lincoln the power of persistence and the link between attitude and altitude.

Let me share with you several ways I think attitude can make a difference in the business world, no matter what the pundits, academics, regulators, or analysts are saying. This has become my personal platform for success.

First, make bold choices and find something—a program, a service, a neighborhood—that really matters to you.

When you find something that really matters to you, you find a way to accomplish a goal. Strangely, it may not be the goal people think you should have. In fact, it may be different from anything you've ever pursued—and at a much lower salary. After all, Albert Schweitzer gave up a lucrative medical practice to spend his time caring for the natives of Africa. Helen Keller, though blind and deaf, dedicated her life to helping people. And Benjamin Disraeli was a Jew at a time when anti-Semitism was running rampant in his country. Yet that didn't keep him from becoming prime minister of England. Each of these people found a goal that mattered and made a life-changing choice. This choice made a difference for others.

Second, do what you've set out to do.

When I look at the people I've admired in my lifetime—and I think about what I've been proudest of in my own life—success came because of a commitment, giving all to achieve a goal. Perhaps it's maintaining a wonderful marriage for more than

217

thirty-five years, as I've done, seeing my two children grow up, and now having the pleasure of watching three grandsons develop and a magazine flourish. Or maybe it's creating a new service for your customers. It doesn't matter what it is—or whether you do it in your home or church, on a neighborhood block, or in the national media.

I thought about commitment recently when I read a statement by the English playwright George Bernard Shaw and was able to relate it to an event I'd seen portrayed in the news. This is what he said: "I'm convinced that my life belongs to the whole community, and as long as I live, it's my privilege to do whatever I can." Shaw told people that he looked at life not as a candle, but as a torch he would hold for a moment, until it burned brightly, and then pass it on to the next generation.

A beautiful image of commitment took root on January 14, 1996, while I was watching the CBS news program *Sunday Morning*. In a wonderful story on the perils of downsizing, a CEO in his seventies, whose plant had burnt to the ground, was addressing his workers for the second time within sixty days. Even though the CEO realized it might be a year before the company could rebuild, he had decided to pay his workers' salaries for a second thirty days.

At a time when few people know if they'll even have a job tomorrow, his blue-collar workers—some of whom had lived in that town for their entire lives—applauded him and wept with gratitude. "I can't abandon these people," said the CEO, choking back tears. "I have to do what's right for them and my community."

And here's my third piece of advice: Turn into the type of person you can respect.

There's a story about a wealthy man who summoned his servant and told him that he was leaving the country for a year, and that while he was gone, he wanted his servant to build a new house. The wealthy man told him to build it well, and that when he returned, he would pay for all the materials and labor. Of course, once the employer left, the servant decided it was foolish to work so hard.

218

So he cut corners and squandered the money he saved. When his employer came back, he paid the bills as he had promised and then asked his servant, "Are you satisfied with the house you built?" When the servant answered that he was, the employer replied, "Good. The house is yours. You can live in it for the rest of your life."

And now, I ask you: If your life—your self—is a house, are you building the kind of place you would be proud to live in forever? Or are you cutting corners just as the servant did, squandering time and commitments? One writer said it well: "If you refuse to accept anything but the best, you very often get it."

For me, turning into the kind of person you can respect means getting back to basics. It means taking responsibility for what you say and do—even what you think. It means keeping your word, delivering on your promises, and being faithful to your spouse, family, and work. It means setting your own internal standards and not comparing yourself to others. And it means not worrying about who gets the credit, but getting the job done.

Being a person you can respect also means having the quiet confidence to do what's right and not waver from a decision even when you come under fire. It means having what some people call the courage of one's convictions.

Late in his life, when Winston Churchill was still Britain's prime minister, he attended an official ceremony. Several rows behind him, two men whispered: "That's Winston Churchill," the men said in hushed tones. "They say he's getting senile. They say he should step aside and leave the country to a younger man." Churchill didn't turn around, but when the ceremony ended, he stopped where the two men were seated, leaned forward, and said, "Gentlemen, they also say he's deaf."

Like all great leaders in politics, business, and religion, Churchill learned the one great secret of being a person worthy of respect: Choose a course of action based not on what's expedient or hot or trendy, but on what's right. Then, when you're sure you've made the right decision, never waver from that course—no matter how much you come under fire.

219

Fourth, fulfill your potential.

Decide once and for all that you'll try to be the best you can be at whatever you do. Vince Lombardi, the legendary coach of the Green Bay Packers, once gave this message to his team: "After the cheers have died and the stadium is empty, after the headlines have been written, and after you are back in the quiet of your own room and the Super Bowl ring has been placed on the dresser and all the promo and fanfare have faded, the enduring things that are left are a dedication to excellence, the dedication to victory, and the satisfaction of doing with our lives the very best we can to make the world a better place to live."

If you want the kind of happiness and deep personal satisfaction that no layoff, economic downturn, or earthquake can destroy, search until you find something you can do best, what no one could pay you enough money not to do, something you would gladly pay for the privilege of doing. Adlai Stevenson was a lot like Lincoln in many ways—intelligent, thoughtful, and verbal— but he never got to be president. Still, he left us some words I'll never forget: "So live—decently, fearless, joyously—and don't forget that in the long run it's not the years in your life, but the life in your years that really counts."

Fifth, learn to enjoy the process of life, not just the rewards.

We live in a goal-oriented society and work in goal-oriented businesses. And, in most cases, it has to be that way. The problem is that most of us want what we want when we want it. Three-minute oatmeal, one-hour dry cleaning, instant success. We want to arrive so badly that we lose sight of what's happening to us in the process of getting there.

Over the years, in my many lines of work, I've learned that it pays to enjoy the process of life, not just its rewards. To me that means living one day at a time, savoring the little victories, and realizing that life is a journey in finding happiness and discovering who you are. It means knowing that just as Rome wasn't built in a day, neither are a career or a family or a life that's worth living. It means taking time to play with my dog, baby-sit with my grandkids, eat pizza with my wife, compliment my secretary,

Cathy, let the other guy get in front of me when I'm driving home, and encourage the great reporters, editors, and ad reps who work with me at *Modern Healthcare.*

An eighty-five-year-old woman probably said it best—and her words may make you think of what you'll say in twenty, thirty, or forty years when you look back on your own life: "I was one of those people who never went anywhere without a thermometer, hot-water bottle, raincoat, and parachute. But if I had my life to live over, I would go barefoot earlier in the spring. I would ride more merry-go-rounds. I would have fewer imaginary troubles. I would take more chances, and I would eat more ice cream." I don't know about eating more ice cream, but I know one thing: At the end of life, few people say they would have worked harder.

My wonderful managing editor, Karen Petite, once collapsed in our offices from a serious case of flu. We immediately called her husband, who works for the city of Chicago. Karen was lying on the couch in my office when her husband, who had left work to be with her, walked into the room. Her face brightened immediately, and in her eyes you could see the look of love mixed with relief. Her husband told her how much he loved her and kissed her tenderly. He could have contracted her illness, but at that moment it didn't seem to matter. He cared more about his wife's well-being than about his own health. And that, for me, was a perfect moment, a moment that captured the essence of life.

So the question I have for you is this: What are you doing to savor life's special moments and miracles? In your push for success and innovation, are you taking time to smell the roses and enjoy other people? If not, I suggest you consider making that a priority.

Sixth, never stop asking questions and opening yourself up to the pain of others.

There's a story about hard times related to me by Jack Sommars, an executive vice president with U S WEST, although the story did not involve U S WEST. The story tells how an employee stood up nervously after a teleconference and asked her company's CEO what advice he could give to help her and others get through the pain of downsizing. The CEO gave a pat executive answer—something about individual responsibility and open communication. But you could tell from the employee's reaction that the CEO's words just hadn't registered.

Then something strange and powerful happened. Almost as an aside, the executives asked the employee what she thought. Without hesitation, the employee looked at the corporate leaders on the podium and reminded them: "We need to be recognized and appreciated," she said. "We need to be told that we're important, that we make a difference. When we're hurting and mourning our friends who are gone, it's important to remember that we're all human beings with feelings."

When she finished—in dozens of U.S. conference rooms across fourteen states—people were wiping their eyes. In some of those rooms, she got a standing ovation. Just about everyone felt better because someone had verbalized their pain and their need for a pat on the back and a kind word.

So perhaps communicating with people in this tough time of downsizing isn't as difficult as we might think. While executives were wringing their hands and analyzing their data in the incident above, an employee delivered the answer. She had it all along. All they had to do was ask.

Finally, devote yourself to something bigger and develop a faith in something or someone larger than yourself.

You may disagree with me, but I think you miss out on a lot if you decide to live life easily or totally for yourself. The highest motives in life are the ones that make us reach out to others. Just ask the Albert Schweitzers or Mother Teresas. And that's why it's important to think about our view of success.

Maybe success shouldn't be measured by what you are, but by what you *could be*—not by what you've done, but what you *could have done*. After a concert, a brilliant musician was greeted by an eager fan. "Oh, I'd give my life to play like you." The musician replied, "I did."

What makes people extraordinary? I personally believe that God works with ordinary people and makes them extraordinary when they show their willingness to dedicate themselves to something larger and more magnificent than they are. I've never been a great reader of poetry, but I cherish four lines written by Longfellow:

> Lives of great people remind us
> We can make our lives sublime,
> And, departing, leave behind us
> Footprints in the sands of time.

And now in this time when angels are getting a lot of attention, I'd like to leave you with a little story. Somewhere long ago and far away, God was thinking about giving the human race the secret of life. So like any good CEO, God called a meeting of the angels. And even though the angels had budgets to prepare and deadlines to meet, they decided to show up. God's question was simple: Where do we hide this gift so that only the nicest, most dedicated people will find it?

The angels couldn't agree. One thought it should be at the bottom of the sea and another thought it should be deep in the earth. Still another thought it should sit on top of a mountain, close to the sky. But a fourth angel had an even better idea.

"People are strange," the fourth angel said. "You never know what they're going to do. Some of them can't swim, so they won't go in the water. Others are claustrophobic, so we should forget about putting it in the earth. And if they're afraid of heights, then they will never climb a mountain. We should place the secret somewhere where people would never dream of looking—inside themselves."

You possess the most precious gift right inside you. Success and happiness in any area of life are a matter of attitude. And that gift—your attitude—lies within.

Life is a series of choices. We have the freedom to choose—every day—between kindness and cruelty, immediate reward and long-term gain, hope and despair. We can even influence other people's choices. But the No. 1 choice, the choice that determines all other choices, is the attitude and approach to living and business we choose for ourselves.

223

The choice of attitude belongs to each person. How high do you want to soar? Do you want to reach for the stars?

They're within your grasp.

When you reach for excellence, reach for the stars...

Chuck Lauer is a motivator who has made it happen. In *Reach for the Stars*, he provides us with some very practical lessons and advice about success, leadership, sales, and customer service. I am always learning from him. This book is another learning experience.

—C. William Pollard
The ServiceMaster Company

The road to success is always under construction. *Reach for the Stars* is full of thoughtful and time-tested advice on how to be, and act like, a true winner. Chuck Lauer has covered every key aspect of what it takes to "successfully" reach for the stars.

—Terry J. Mulligan
Baxter International

Everyone has experienced episodes when business is lousy, competitors are attacking from all angles, employees are grousing, and it seems like time to throw in the towel. That's the ideal time to pick up Chuck Lauer's *Reach for the Stars* because *Reach for the Stars* will pick you up. Here is a wealth of instructive and inspirational material to give you a new, upbeat take on business—and life. A must-read for all of us.

—Joe Cappo
Crain Communications Inc.

Reach for the Stars

Here's an opportunity to impact your associates in a positive way at a publisher-direct price. *Reach for the Stars* embraces Chuck Lauer's practical wisdom and insight.

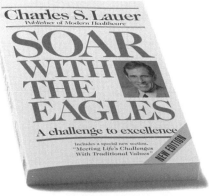

"If you want to soar with the

eagles...

in the business world, Charles S. Lauer's new book may become the wind beneath your wings.... Mr. Lauer, publisher of *Modern Healthcare* magazine, packs his own brand of enthusiasm, excitement, and charisma into every page. This is an ambitious, well-rounded book for business people at all levels who want to widen and strengthen their wingspan."

—Sandra Pesman
Business Marketing magazine

"Lauer...confronts core issues facing us today with facts, wit, enthusiasm, and refreshing frankness and brevity.... Lauer's positive—even humorous—presentation of the basics of good business has inspired me and members of our staff to change the way we do some things in and away from the office."

—Bruce F. Trumm III
Business Director, New Direction, Columbus, Ohio

"*Soar With the Eagles* is filled with the type of insightful information that can benefit anyone, in any profession. It's inspiring but not preachy, provocative yet unpretentious."

—Mike Leonard
Feature Reporter, NBC News
Correspondent, *Today* show

Here's an opportunity to impact your associates in a positive way at a publisher-direct price. *Soar With the Eagles* embraces Chuck Lauer's practical wisdom and insight; it's bound to be a favorite book in every personal library. Order your copies today!

Soar With the Eagles
Publisher-direct corporate gift pricing

Per-copy prices, plus shipping and handling

Single copy		$11.95 each
2-10 copies	10% off	10.76 each
11-50 copies	20% off	9.56 each
51-250 copies	30% off	8.37 each
251+ copies	40% off	7.17 each

Invite your friends on a journey to excellence.

**Call your order to
1-800-952-9089
Or fax your order to
1-509-525-0281**

ORDER FORM

Soar With the Eagles

☐ Please send me _____ copies of *Soar With the Eagles* at the per-copy price quoted in the price table above (plus shipping).

To expedite your order,
CALL: 1-800-952-9089
FAX: 1-509-525-0281

☐ I want to receive a review copy of *Soar With the Eagles* at $11.95 plus $4 shipping and handling.

☐ Payment enclosed. (Make checks payable to CCI Books.) In Washington state, add 7.8% sales tax.

☐ Charge my credit card: ☐ MasterCard   ☐ VISA

Card number _____ _____ _____ _____ Expiration date _____

Authorized signature_____ Date _____

☐ Bill me (plus shipping). My purchase order number _____

Name: Mr./Ms._____

Title _____ Organization _____

Address _____

City _____ State _____ ZIP _____